Pentecost Comes to Church

Pentecost Comes to Church

Sacraments and Spiritual Gifts

JOHN GUNSTONE

DARTON · LONGMAN + TODD

First published in 1994 by
Darton, Longman and Todd Ltd
1 Spencer Court
140–142 Wandsworth High Street
London SW18 4JJ

ISBN 0–232–52045–3

A catalogue record for this book is available
from the British Library

Thanks are due to Church House Publishing for permission to quote
from *Patterns for Worship*; SCM Press Ltd for permission to
quote from John A. T. Robinson, *The Body* and Alan Richardson,
An Introduction to the Theology of the New Testament; Thankyou
Music, P.O. Box 75, Eastbourne BN23 6NW for songs from *Songs
and Hymns of Fellowship*.

The Scripture quotations in this publication are from *The New
International Version*, copyright 1973, 1978, 1984 by International Bible
Society, published by Hodder & Stoughton

Phototypeset by Intype, London
Printed and bound in Great Britain
by Redwood Books, Trowbridge, Wiltshire

Contents

Preface

This book is about the relationship between the sacraments and spiritual gifts in the light of our experience of the charismatic renewal. The topic has not, as far as I know, been discussed much among Anglicans.

The book begins with an account of the origins of the Pentecostal and charismatic movements, with particular reference to those teachings and practices which influence our experience and understanding of the sacraments. Then baptism, confirmation, the eucharist, the ordained ministry and other sacramental signs are reviewed against this background, with some reference to their historical development. Finally, I have made a few suggestions about the lessons to be drawn from the discussion for the life and mission of the Church of England.

I have restricted what I have written to my own Church because otherwise the discussion would have become unmanageable. I would have had to qualify everything I said to take account of the differing (though now converging) views of the sacraments in the various Church denominations, and the result would have been over-complicated. But Baptists, Methodists, United Reformed members, Roman Catholics and others should not have much difficulty in transposing matters I have raised to their own situations. We all face the same questions. And we need each other's help in seeking the Holy Spirit's guidance towards the right answers, as I hope I've made clear.

JOHN GUNSTONE
Easter Day, 1994

1

Holiness and Pentecostal Movements

Nearly half a billion Christians on this planet are either Pente-costals or Charismatics.

Whatever we think of statistics – give or take a few millions – that is an amazing figure. Especially when we recall that before the year 1900 Pentecostal churches did not exist.

Such a statistic signals that we in the Church of England, as well as those in other denominations, must engage with Pentecostal experiences and teachings to learn what God may be revealing to us through them. If the prophetic Spirit is to be found in *some* aspects of Pentecostalism, then we must discern what he is showing us, particularly – for the purposes of this discussion – in our understanding of the sacraments.

At first, Pentecostals do not appear to have much in common with sacramentalist Christians. What could they contribute to our Anglican teaching on infant baptism, or the eucharist, or the threefold ministry of bishops, priests and deacons?

But appearances can be misleading. Pentecostalism stemmed from the Holiness movements of the nineteenth century at about the same time that Anglicans were rediscovering, through the Tractarians and their successors, the grace of the sacraments. Both the Holiness-Pentecostal and the ritualist movements were responding to the impulses of the Holy Spirit leading God's people to be more faithful disciples of Jesus Christ – in other words, to be truly sanctified. Catholic Anglicans took their inspiration from the high church tradition of the past and from contemporary Roman Catholicism. Holiness-Pentecostals took their inspiration from the evangelical revivals which swept North America and parts of Europe from the time of John Wesley and Jonathan Edwards. Both had the same objective – to lead Christians into greater holiness.

When asked about their beginnings, Pentecostals say their movement was born in Azusa Street, Los Angeles, in 1906, when the Spirit fell on a congregation of poor whites and blacks. The revival was a Californian spiritual earthquake which had seismic effects all over the Christian world. Since the wooden chapel in Azusa Street had apparently once been a farm building, Pentecostals could claim that their movement had been 'born in a stable'.

It's a good story. In this century of struggle for civil rights in the United States of America, the tale underscores the truth that the Spirit creates unity between whites and blacks in Jesus Christ. But as historians of the movement are researching into their forefathers' lives, a revisionist interpretation of Pentecostal origins is taking place. It is now realised that, while the events in Azusa Street caught the imagination of the Christian public, they were part of a widespread and diverse movement which emerged out of the Holiness churches and swept different parts of the USA in the first years of this century.

One of the key figures was Charles Fox Parham (1873–1929). Although it is an exaggeration to claim he was the founder of Pentecostalism, nevertheless his reinterpretation of Holiness teaching on 'baptism in the Spirit' became one of its basic tenets.

Parham was born in Muscatine, Iowa. When he was five, his parents moved to Cheney, Kansas. His mother, to whom he was closely attached, trained him in commitment to Jesus Christ and evangelical piety. She died when he was twelve. Deeply grieved, he used to say he would meet her again one day in heaven, and he determined to live to that end.

Plagued with ill-health as a youth, he experienced several remarkable recoveries which gave him a sense that God was preparing him for a ministry of divine healing. His faith in this vocation was so strong that he refused medicines and would not take out a health insurance. Belief in miraculous healings and rejection of scientific medicine were features of early Pentecostalism.

From the Holiness preachers who came to the church he attended he learned the doctrine of sanctification as second work of grace. This expectation of a deep work of the Spirit in the believer came from the Wesleyan roots of the Holiness tradition. It convinced Parham and other early Pentecostal leaders that divine sanctification was available to all Christians if they opened themselves to the Lord.

Parham went to college in Kansas to prepare for what he believed his ministry was to be. There he learned doctrines of healing in the atonement, dispensational premillennialism, and baptism in the Spirit as an empowering to serve the Lord and live a godly life. He became acquainted with the establishment of Bible schools, homes of healing, religious periodicals, and inner-city social work.

He married in 1896 and, after two or three years as a pastor, he and his wife established a home of healing in Topeka, Kansas. In 1900 he went on a tour of Holiness centres and it was in one of these, a Christian commune at Shiloh, Maine, that he sought baptism in the Spirit for himself. Here he encountered speaking in tongues. He also read a report of how one of the Shiloh community, a young lady named Jennie Glassey, had spoken in an African dialect after receiving a missionary call to Africa.

This tale made a great impression on him. Believing that Christ's premillennial return would occur on the heels of a worldwide revival, he concluded that the spiritual gift of speaking in tongues was being restored to those who were baptised in the Spirit to make them instant missionaries – able to preach the gospel in any language anywhere in the world in preparation for Christ's coming. He was apparently not then aware of the distinction between xenolalia (speaking in a known tongue) and glossalalia (speaking in an unknown tongue). The encounter with the commune confirmed what he had read in Acts 2, and he took it as a sign that the end-time was approaching.

The New Year in Topeka

Returning to Topeka, Kansas, Parham founded the Bethel Bible School to prepare prospective missionaries for the eschatological outpouring of the Spirit. In an old mansion on the edge of the town he taught his thirty or so students to 'pray in' each passage of the Scriptures. According to Parham's later accounts, he left his students at the end of 1900 to go on a speaking engagement, setting them the task of discovering the evidence for the reception of the Spirit from the Scriptures. He then told how at midnight on 31 December 1900 one of them, Agnes Ozman, received the gift of tongues during a watchnight service and, when he returned, he found that many of his students had been baptised in the Spirit.

In the popular history of the Pentecostal churches, this dramatic event is interpreted as a sign that at the beginning of the new century God was doing a new thing among his people. But the revisionists have been correcting the details. History shows that it was Parham himself who led his students to see that tongues for mission was the New Testament evidence for baptism in the Spirit during his lecture on 1 January 1901. Parham was not the last Charismatic to embroider the story of the pioneer years of his ministry as his memory of them became misty!

Some of his students went out to spread the message that God was restoring his Church in its apostolic Pentecostal power. They joined numerous other bands of Holiness preachers and missioners who, at considerable personal cost and self-sacrifice, preached this message in the towns of Kansas, Missouri and Texas.

Members of the Apostolic Faith mission, they were extremely creative in their tactics and strategy – meetings and parades in streets, dramatic preachings, prayer for the sick, camp meetings, printed leaflets and periodicals, short-term Bible schools. The message gained recruits among the common folk, including ethnic minorities. Women were prominent in the movement, not only in leading the singing but also in preaching and in ministry to the sick. It all sounds familiar to those of us who in recent years have been involved in Marches for Jesus, charismatic rallies, ministries of healing, holiday conferences like New Wine, magazines and handouts, and courses run by renewal service agencies and parishes.

Parham's own preaching, though sensational, was a strange compost of Holiness doctrines mingled with ideas about conditional mortality, baptism in the Spirit as a sign of the second coming before the rapture, Zionism, divine healing, and prophetic discourses arising out of current events and pseudo-science. Perhaps we should not be shocked that he also adopted without question the racial prejudices of contemporary American society. When a black man named Seymour joined his Bible school, which by then had moved to Houston, Parham had no hesitation in applying the rules governing the segregation of whites and blacks in Texas. He would not allow Seymour to sit in the room with the white students – the black man had to listen to Parham's lectures outside the door. Most other Christian teachers in the Deep South would have regarded that as normal then.

The story of early Pentecostalism now switches to this black student. William James Seymour (1870–1922) was the son of former slaves from Centerville, Louisiana. He had taught himself to read and write before he enrolled as a student in Parham's Bible School. He accepted unreservedly Parham's teaching that speaking in tongues was the New Testament sign of baptism in the Spirit.

After leaving the school early in 1906, he was invited to preach at a Holiness church in Los Angeles. His views on speaking in tongues were so divisive, however, that he was not allowed in the church again. Eventually he found a building which had formerly been used by an African Methodist Episcopal church in Azusa Street, and it was there in April of that year that he began a ministry which made him a catalyst in publicising Pentecostalism.

The revival at Azusa Street owed much to what was then the recent development of communications, not only in the USA but across the Atlantic. The invention of the telegraph meant that newspapers could print news while it was still hot; and it was the news of what was happening in that little church which drew thousands of people to it.

They came from everywhere: sceptics, seekers, and church leaders alike from different countries, people of all colours and classes. White bishops and black workers, men and women, Asians and Mexicans, white professors and black laundry women visited the church during those few years. The overshadowing of the Spirit was so powerful that no one queried the leadership of a black man, or the assistance given to him by a number of black and white women. Everyone sensed a form of racial and sexual equality as brothers and sisters seeking the Lord together.

What touched many was the experience of an immanent God. This contrasted sharply with what they heard in the sermons of their own churches, where transcendence was the dominant theme. Those early Pentecostals expected to experience divine power in prophecies, tongues, healings, and other manifestations; and at the meetings in Azusa Street these expectations

were not disappointed. Visitors went away believing divine
power was immediately available now for the faithful and Spirit-
filled disciples of Jesus Christ.

The Spreading Flame

The astonishing thing about this revival was that, although it
lasted only a few years (by 1915 the congregation numbered a
handful), its effect was felt in so many parts of the world in the
decades which followed. Even now historians are discovering
fresh links between individuals and families who once attended
meetings at Azusa Street and the planting and growth of Pentecostal churches in different countries.

But it was not just within Pentecostal churches that the
message spread. Those who were touched by the revival
belonged to many different denominations and traditions, and
the theological themes of personal salvation, holiness, divine
healing, baptism in the Spirit with power for ministry, and the
return of the Lord, provided ample motivation to ensure that
the revival had a long-term impact.

Within a few years Pentecostalism began to lose its initial
dynamism. Some of the early leaders of the movement were
neurotically individualist, liable to compete with one another
in attracting followers, and suspicious of anything that
resembled an unholy organisation. Divisiveness (including
racism), lack of co-ordination, wild claims for spurious spiritual
manifestations, premillenial hopes raised and dashed – plenty
went wrong. Nevertheless, the spread of the movement is
impressive. At the centre of it was the conviction which Parham
and Seymour did so much to popularise, that baptism in the
Spirit with the gift of tongues was a sign that the believer was
being empowered to preach the gospel.

By the twenties and thirties North American Pentecostal
churches had become like many other evangelical, middle-class
congregations, with ecclesiastical bureaucracies and theological
seminaries. Pentecostal churches in this country attracted
mainly the working classes. But the real spirit of the movement
flowed back into black Pentecostalism. In Central and Latin
America, in Africa, and in countries of the Asian subcontinent,
this form of Christianity retained and developed the vitality

of its origins and resulted in the appearance of thousands of indigenous churches around the world.

Then eventually the Pentecostal expectation of baptism in the Spirit penetrated the traditional denominations, first the Anglican and Reformed Churches, then the Roman Catholic Church, and then more recently some of the Orthodox Churches.

But before we leave this story, however, we should note certain things.

1. At the heart of Pentecostal spirituality is the experience of 'baptism in the Holy Spirit' with the manifestation of speaking in tongues. Pentecostal churches vary in their understanding of how this Spirit-baptism, as they call it, is appropriated – from the Oneness Pentecostal stream (who baptise only in the name of Jesus Christ) to the Latter Rain groups (who believe that the outpouring of the Spirit is the 'latter rain' of Joel 2:28 KJV heralding the imminent return of the Lord) – so that it would be more accurate to speak of Pentecostal *traditions*.

But they all teach baptism in the Spirit. Without Spirit-baptism, they say, Christians have not received all that is offered us by God. For them Jesus should be preached in the Church and in the world as 'Saviour', 'Baptiser with the Holy Spirit', 'Physician' and 'Coming King'. If Christ is presented with any of those four titles missing, then the gospel is not proclaimed 'full' or 'four-square'. The term 'Full Gospel' is a typical Pentecostal title. The Pentecostal Fellowship of North America affirms, 'We believe that the full Gospel includes holiness of heart and life, healing for the body, and baptism in the Holy Spirit with the evidence of speaking in other tongues as the Spirit gives the utterance.'

2. Pentecostals have a strong sense of the Church as the community of active believers. Those baptised in water and the Spirit are expected to exercise spiritual gifts, the charisms. And since the gifts of the Spirit are manifested through the physical creation, the experience gives Pentecostals what might be called a sacramental outlook on Christian ministry. For them outward and visible signs have important inward and spiritual graces.

They hear the voice of God in 'word gifts' such as inspired speech, speaking in tongues, interpretations of tongues, prophecies, words of wisdom and knowledge, and singing in the Spirit.

They see his works in healings and deliverance ministries. They are conscious of his presence in prophetic gestures and praise expressed in body language. They could be said to be sacramentalists in the general sense of that word. This is reinforced by the fact that water, the laying on of hands and anointing with oil, as well as the use of bread and wine at the Lord's Supper, are all accepted as ways in which the Spirit operates among God's people today, following the example of Jesus' ministry and that of the New Testament Church.

Pentecostals have not evolved a sacramental theology as such. On the contrary, they have avoided the use of the word 'sacrament'. But they respect what they call the 'ordinances' of the Lord, and in some churches their discipline in matters such as informal confession of sins and admission to Communion have all the hallmarks of primitive Catholicism.

3. Pentecostal teachers have always stressed the difference between the gifts of the Spirit and the fruit of the Spirit. The exercise of spiritual power, they say, is not necessarily a sign of holiness, though that power can be more effective if it is exercised through a holy life.

They point out that the New Testament teaching on spiritual gifts is associated with sanctification as well as with ministry. The exposition of the charisms in 1 Corinthians 12 and 14 encloses Paul's teaching on the primacy of love in chapter 13. The same pattern is found in Romans 12, Ephesians 4–5 and 1 Peter 4:8–11. Pentecostalism is about spiritual power for evangelism; but it is even more about scriptural holiness.

4. In its early days Pentecostalism was ecumenical. Many of the original leaders did not want to set up new churches. They had a vision of all existing churches being Spirit-filled and becoming partners in preaching the gospel in preparation for the second Advent.

The Azusa Street mission statement proclaimed, 'The Apostolic Faith movement stands for Christian Unity everywhere.' Their ecumenical charity may not have stretched to embrace Roman Catholics, but they were remarkably open to all Christians, even Episcopalians. Baptism in the Spirit gave Pentecostals a yearning for unity among those whom they discerned were true disciples of Jesus Christ.

That vision was delayed in coming. During the first fifty years of this century Pentecostals have been marginalised by other denominations. It was only in the sixties that they began to attract the interest of those in other churches. And much of that was due to the extraordinary, globe-trotting ministry of the Pentecostal teacher, David du Plessis (1905–87), who for thirty years visited Christians of other denominations, sharing with them his insights into the working of the Holy Spirit.

Pentecostalism has now become the great third stream alongside Catholicism and Protestantism in the contemporary Christian world. Some of their churches have become members of the World Council of Churches. Those in the traditional denominations who began to learn from them were particularly interested in the Pentecostal teaching and practice of baptism in the Spirit and the exercise of the gifts of the Spirit (the *charismata* of 1 Corinthians 12:4). Hence they came to be known as 'Charismatics' and collectively as 'the charismatic renewal'.[1]

I must now sketch how that renewal spread into the Church of England.

2

Renewing Anglicans

Only a few individual members of the Church of England had personal contacts with Pentecostals in the first half of this century. In the parish of All Saints, Monkwearmouth, in the Durham diocese, the vicar, the Revd Alexander Boddy (1854–1930), was baptised in the Holy Spirit during a visit to Pentecostal churches in Sweden in 1907. For years afterwards he hosted the annual Pentecostal Convention at Sunderland and edited the Pentecostal periodical *Confidence* from 1908 to 1926. But for the most Anglicans in this country the Assemblies of God and the Elim Pentecostal Church were regarded as outside their ecumenical interest or concern.

It was not until the fifties that Pentecostal spirituality began to touch them. When it did, it was a Catholic Anglican who responded to it first – William Wood ('Brother Bill'), warden of the London Healing Mission. The LHM stressed the importance of a sacramental ministry to the sick, and it was the Pentecostal expectation of the gift of healing which attracted the warden's attention.

In his newsletters Brother Bill wrote he was certain that what he called a 'Pentecost of the Twentieth Century' was emerging. Through his friendship with Agnes Sanford, the wife of an Episcopalian priest, who did much to promote the ministry of healing in this country as well as in the USA, he experienced inner healing and baptism in the Spirit himself, though he did not speak in tongues. Peter Hocken, who has chronicled these events in *Streams of Renewal* (1986), thinks Brother Bill was the first member of any mainline church in Britain to recognise that there was a Pentecost-type movement *outside* the Pentecostal churches. Brother Bill found he now had a new expectancy of charisms of healing in his sacrament-based ministry to the sick and troubled.

What was then called 'Neo-Pentecostalism' first spread in

any depth among Catholic Anglicans in the Episcopal Church of the USA. The story of how one Sunday in 1959 the Revd Dennis Bennett announced to his congregation at the parish communion in St Mark's Church, Van Nuys, California, that he had been baptised in the Spirit and spoken in tongues, has now passed into the legends of the Anglican charismatic renewal. But Peter says that another priest, Richard Winkler, rector of Trinity Episcopal Church in Wheaton, was baptised in the Spirit three years previously. Many of the other Episcopalians who were blessed in those early years became leaders in the renewal, like Charles ('Chuck') Irish, Everett ('Terry') Fullam and Graham Pulkingham.

In England the renewal spread mostly among Evangelical Anglicans. The church press recorded one or two of the more sensational early events – such as when a student at what was then Clifton Theological College in Bristol was expelled because he was supposed to have been teaching others to speak in tongues. St Mark's, Gillingham, St Mark's, Cheltenham, and St Paul's, Beckenham, all received publicity for outbreaks of 'tongues' in the years 1962–4.

Michael Harper was a curate of All Souls, Langham Place, London, when he decided in 1964 to form the Fountain Trust to promote understanding of what was happening. Although ecumenical in its aims, the Fountain Trust was supported mainly by Evangelical Anglicans at first. I attended one of the early charismatic conferences organised by the Trust at Stoke Poges that same year. Of the twenty-one people present, seventeen were clergy of the Church of England: fifteen were Evangelicals; Michael Meakin and I were the only Catholic Anglicans.

The Church of England first reacted to the charismatic renewal with suspicion and incredulity – suspicion, because it sensed that the movement might be elitist and divisive; incredulity, because it assumed Charismatics could not be anything other than theologically naive or emotionally disturbed. But the renewal continued to spread throughout the seventies. Certain parishes emerged as models of what might happen when its lessons were applied pastorally. Some of these became famous through the wider ministry of their clergy – notably St Michael-le-Belfry, York, under David Watson's leadership.

Gradually the feeling grew that the Church of England should make some sort of official response to what was happening

among its members. The opportunity for this arose when Colin
Buchanan, then principal of St John's College, Nottingham,
placed before the General Synod in 1978 a motion calling for
a report which would 'explore the reasons for this upsurge,
pinpoint the particular distinctive features of spirituality and
ethos which the movement presents, and indicate both the
points of tension which exist within traditional Anglicanism and
also how the riches of the movement may be conserved for the
good of the Church.'

A small working party was formed. I was invited to join it.
We consulted widely and invited parishes to send us comments
on the effect of the renewal in their life and worship. The
material flowed in and we had several meetings to digest it and
to exchange stories and ideas. Colin, who was also a member,
drafted sections of our report. Source critics, reading it today,
will not have much difficulty in detecting the passages of breezy
Buchananese among its sixty-six pages.

The Charismatic Movement in the Church of England was
published in 1981. It pointed out that as early as 1953 Lesslie
Newbigin, in *The Household of God*, had said Christians must
learn to distinguish three streams within the worldwide Church
– not just Catholicism and Protestantism but also Pentecostalism. 'The oddity which Newbigin did not foretell,' the report
said, '(though his whole argument points ideally towards it) is
that the Pentecostal experience has been found *within* the Catholic and Protestant traditions, and not just complementing them
from the outside' (p. 44).

After sketching the origins of Pentecostalism, the report
listed what it saw as the particular values of the renewal –
encouragement to prayer, loosening up of worship, development of the healing ministry, strengthening of ecumenical
relationships – and briefly noted without much discussion Pentecostal teaching on baptism in the Spirit and charisms such as
tongues and prophecy.

In attempting to answer why the charismatic renewal was
spreading in the Church of England, various suggestions were
put forward: the appeal of the book of Acts as a model of what
a Christian community should be; a lack of an experience of
God's presence and power in much of Anglican Church life; a
reaction against an over-clericalised institution; a protest against
an over-cerebral approach to faith; an escape from formalism;

and a realisation that the New Testament has much more to teach about the work of the Holy Spirit in the individual and in the Church than is usually realised among Anglicans (in theological terms, the Church of England had an 'impoverished pneumatology').

The report ended by urging Charismatics and non-Charismatics to continue learning from one another and to avoid giving the impression that there were first- and second-class Christians in the Church.

Worship and Cross-fertilisation

Rereading the report recently after a lapse of more than a dozen years, it struck me that we said practically nothing about the impact of the charismatic renewal on the sacramental teaching and practices of the Church of England. I do not remember that this issue was raised during the meetings of the working party.

We received many letters from parishes referring to the ministry of healing (i.e., prayer offered either in groups or in services with the laying on of hands) as one of the signs of the renewal. The report has an appendix which lists the use of the phrase 'baptism in the Holy Spirit' in the New Testament, discusses briefly the relationship between it and the rites of initiation, and concludes that the charismatic experience does not justify anyone being given a second or rebaptism. But it said nothing else on the sacraments. The report did, however, make two other references which are relevant to our discussion.

1. In describing the greater freedom experienced in worship, with the use of body-language, music, artwork, movement, colour, and in the celebration of the eucharist itself, the report suggested that these features are a form of sacramentalism in the widest sense of that word. It called this 'inchoate sacramentality' – that is, a germ of sacramentalism which promises future development. 'As with so many other features of this renewal, this change comes ... by a new contagious practice infecting the practitioners with new "gut-level" understanding of the created order and its role in our approach to God and his to us' (p. 37).

2. In a section called 'Cross-fertilisation' the report drew

attention to the greater understanding which Anglicans of different theological persuasions developed towards one another as a result of baptism in the Spirit – including views on the sacraments.

It is likely that charismatic renewal brings missing dimensions to some of the existing traditions of the Church. To the Evangelical, it brings a release from negative attitudes to sacramentalism and the created order. Cartoon puritanism is swept aside, and a healthy reform of worship is set in hand. The Evangelical may also be delivered from his fear of Rome, and thus share in worship and activities with Roman Catholic charismatics, on a basis of true mutual acceptance rather than fierce hostility. (p. 39)

Although the report was commended by only a narrow majority in the General Synod, it was widely read and for some weeks it was among the best-sellers in religious bookshops. I visited a number of diocesan and deanery synods to introduce it.

On these occasions I usually arranged with a local guitar group to end the proceedings with a half-hour of what I called 'charismatic prayer'. Among the choruses and spontaneous prayers (and occasionally a gift of tongues) I was careful to include elements from the *Alternative Service Book*'s form of Evening Prayer. At the end, before I said goodbye, I would ask those present if they could name the kind of service we had just had. A few would mumble something about 'a charismatic prayer meeting' or – more sceptically – 'a chorus sandwich'. I enjoyed watching their reactions when I pointed out that they had just been to an ASB Evensong!

To follow up the report and to help parishes which were struggling to relate the renewal to their life and worship, Anglican Renewal Ministries was formed with Lawrence Hoyle as its first director (he was succeeded in 1988 by Michael Mitton). ARM's conferences and courses (notably *Saints Alive!*) did much in the succeeding years to spread the lessons of the renewal.[1]

After the publication of the Synod report, attitudes in the Church of England began to change. Many came to realise that, far from being a passing fascination, the renewal had taken root and was strengthening the faith of increasing numbers of Anglicans. It was also having a marked impact on the worship,

service and witness of many parishes. A letter went out from
the Archbishops' appointments secretary to diocesan bishops
advising them to ensure that, when filling vacancies, clergy
sympathetic to the charismatic renewal were placed in parishes
where the movement was strong. The proportion of charismatic
students in theological colleges expanded dramatically. By the
end of the eighties it was more than half.

The English Church Census, undertaken by Marc Europe in
1989, shows that between 1985 and 1989 parishes describing
themselves as 'charismatic evangelical' experienced growth of
five per cent or more in thirty-six out of forty-five English
counties, while in another twelve counties membership had
remained static. This was in sharp contrast to the figures for
the Church of England generally, which showed that there had
been growth in only two counties and decline of five per cent
or more in fifteen. Since 1989 the decline has halted and a slight
increase is beginning – though unfortunately this fact has not
yet penetrated the minds of those who control the media.

Between these same years the independent evangelical
churches, including the 'house' or 'new churches' in England
(now about 1,000), nearly all of whom are charismatic, increased
their membership by five per cent or more in every county,
while the Pentecostal churches grew by five per cent in twenty-
seven counties.[2]

Parishes in Renewal

During these years more parishes were openly identified with
the renewal and experimenting with pioneer ministries. St
Thomas Crookes, Sheffield, an Anglican-Baptist local ecumenical project, initiated a form of worship geared to contemporary
youth culture; the principles behind this are being applied elsewhere (the 'Late Late Service' in Glasgow and 'Joy' in Oxford)
and represent a considerable revolution in our understanding
of liturgy. St Andrew's, Chorleywood, a few years ago launched
a summer camp called 'New Wine' in Somerset which currently
draws ten thousand people, a high proportion of them Anglicans. Holy Trinity, Brompton, hosted conferences on church
planting and developed a successful form of evangelistic teach-

ing in its 'Alpha' courses. Other parishes have taken similar initiatives.

Along with these developments, however, there was little theological reflection in Church of England circles on the charismatic renewal in general or of its impact on sacramental doctrine and practice in particular. The Fountain Trust's *Theological Renewal* published one or two articles on baptism and one on the eucharist during its short life. In 1977 a joint statement was issued by a group drawn from members of the Fountain Trust and the Church of England Evangelical Council called *Gospel and Spirit* which included a paragraph about the sacrament of baptism which, it said, is:

> A unitary work of God with many facets . . . expressed by a cluster of partly overlapping concepts, including forgiveness, justification, adoption, regeneration, conversion (embracing repentance and faith in Jesus Christ as Lord and Saviour), a new creation, death, burial and resurrection in and with Christ, and the giving and reception of the Holy Spirit . . . God's initiatory work is itself apprehended and experienced by different individuals in differing ways and time-scales . . . But essentially the concepts all belong together, since together they express the single full reality of the believer's incorporation into Christ, which leads to assurance of sonship, and power to live and serve in Christ. (p. 3)

In the eighties a small group of Evangelical, Catholic and charismatic Anglicans met in the headquarters of the Church Union in London, under the chairmanship of Eric Kemp, Bishop of Chichester. It became known as 'the Faith House group'. I was a member and presented a paper on the eucharist. Responses were made from the Catholic and the Evangelical viewpoints by Maurice Chandler and Roger Beckwith. Some of the material from that paper, amended in the light of their comments, is used in Chapter 13.

After the publication of the Synod report in 1981, there were requests that the influence of Pentecostal theology on the charismatic renewal should be studied. But it was not until 1991 that the Doctrine Commission of the Church of England issued *We believe in the Holy Spirit*. Although this report did not focus on the charismatic renewal, it nevertheless had the movement in mind, though it did not seem to include anyone who had hands on (or perhaps I should say hands up!) experience of the renewal. It had little to say about the relationship of charisms to sacraments, except in its comments on baptism in the Spirit, which I shall discuss later. The Commission did, however, recognise that the renewal was permeating all the churches and that a deepening of ecumenical relationships was resulting from this. The Commission then went on:

> Unfortunately with that open ecumenical spirit has also gone a decline in historical awareness and in a sense of the Church's Catholicity stretching back over time as well as across denominational barriers. Thus within Anglicanism its classic works of previous centuries are left almost wholly unread at theological colleges, and when there is added to this the very large numbers coming forwards for ordination who are first generation practising Anglicans, the Church of England's current crisis of identity becomes readily explicable. The community jumps from the twentieth century to the first without very much sense of what has gone between, or if it has such a sense, no awareness that the centuries in between have also been an informed part of the Spirit's continuing work. Ironically, even that western denomination which was in the past most concerned about its continuing historical identity displays now a very different face. Even many Roman Catholic theologians write only with reference to the Bible, while the laity now have less awareness of the generations of saints who have made their church what it is. (p. 88)

Although the complaint is made rather peevishly (it reads as if it was written by a resentful Catholic Anglican), it has some justification. I have that weakness in mind in writing this book.

Other Movements of the Spirit

During these years the Church of England was being influenced by other worldwide movements which are signs of the Holy Spirit's activity among God's people. These movements are still continuing.

The first is the restoration of the Bible's authority in preaching, worship and personal devotion. This is remarkable in an age when the Scriptures are subject to so much academic – and highly publicised – questioning. Some would say this is the result of a gulf developing between the biblical theologians and the Church's membership. Others – including myself – would argue that it is the Church's membership who are seeking God's Word and are discovering where that Word is to be found.

I shall not say much about the effect of the renewal on our understanding of the Scriptures. I want to add, however, that the charismatic experience of the Spirit does, for many of us, enhance our sense of both the unchanging authority of the Bible and its measureless capacity to be relevant and applicable in new situations.

The second is the liturgical movement, which has resulted in the production and use of the *Alternative Service Book* in 1980 and the subsequent publications of the Church of England's Liturgical Commission. As we shall see, these services have provided a valuable framework within which the charismatic experience of worship can be expressed with great freedom. The calendar and lectionary were also revised, restoring the feast of Pentecost to its ancient and honoured position as the crown of the Church's year.

The third is the deepening of ecumenical relations among all the major denominations, so that increasingly their members are beginning to think of themselves primarily as Christians and only secondarily as Anglicans, Baptists, Catholics and so on. Charismatics in all the denominations – not least in the Roman Church – are playing an important role in this grassroots movement for unity.

From the viewpoint of charismatic Anglicans, it seems as if God was preparing the way for the renewal in these three movements. And in discussing the relationship between the gifts of the Spirit and sacramental teaching and practice, I shall often refer to them.

Theological reflection on the renewal has been going on elsewhere. The papers of the Roman Catholic-Pentecostal dialogue have been published in the magazine *One in Christ* from 1973 onwards. *Pneuma*, the journal of the Society for Pentecostal Studies, has appeared regularly since 1978. In 1992 the Sheffield Academic Press began publishing the *Journal of Pentecostal Theology*. Anglican Renewal Ministries include a theological paper in their magazine *Anglicans for Renewal*. The

Pentecostals have entered the academic world in force. I have
drawn on all these sources in writing this book.

That sets the scene for our task. Michael Ramsey used to say
that Anglicans liked to do their theology within the sound of
church bells. I think he got that idea from the days when he
was professor of theology at Durham. He used to lecture in a
room on Palace Green, between the cathedral and the castle,
at nine o'clock in the morning, dressed in a cassock and carrying
a surplice, hood and scarf over his arm. When the final bell
rang out from the cathedral for ten o'clock matins, he rushed
across the grass pulling on his robes and joined the line of choir
and canons as they processed up the nave.

For me, it is charismatic prayer meetings which do much
to enlighten my understanding of the gospel. So I venture to
amend Michael Ramsey's dictum and say that, since the administration of the sacraments and the experience of the charisms
have often been associated with worship in my life, I want to
do theology praising God.

3

Baptism in the Spirit

The phrase 'baptism in the Spirit' is, of course, derived from the New Testament's record of John the Baptist's preaching. There was an expectation in Judaea that the coming messianic age would be, among other things, an era of great spiritual power. It was prophesied that the Messiah, when he came, would be equipped by the Spirit to fulfil God's purposes for his people (Isaiah 42:1; 61:1 – fulfilled in Luke 4:18). The new covenant God would establish with them would be in the Spirit (Ezekiel 36:22–32). On that day all God's people would be empowered (Isaiah 44:3; Joel 2:28–9).

These messianic prophecies are fulfilled and exemplified in the New Testament by Jesus. In preparation for Christ's ministry, John the Baptist preached that, in contrast to his own water baptism as a sign of divine forgiveness, the one who would come after him would baptise in the Spirit.

All three synoptic Gospels record this saying. In Mark 1:8 John's words are, 'I baptise you with water, but he will baptise you with (the) Holy Spirit' (the definite article is not in the Greek). Matthew 3:11 and Luke 3:16 add 'with fire', suggesting that the Spirit would come with judgement as well as with power – an eschatological note which influenced Pentecostal preaching.

In the fourth Gospel the Baptist says God told him, 'The man on whom you see the Spirit come down and remain is he who will baptise with the Holy Spirit' (John 1:33). A more literal translation would be, 'This is the (one) baptising (or, baptiser) in Holy Spirit'. In John 1 the Forerunner gives Jesus three titles: the Lamb of God who takes away the sins of the world, the Baptiser in the Spirit, and the Son of God (verses 29, 33 and 34).

The baptism of Jesus was accompanied by a theophany, the descent of the Spirit in the form of a dove and the voice from heaven announcing him to be God's Son. Then Jesus' public ministry began. In his first sermon in the synagogue at Nazareth he declared he had received the Spirit for his ministry, quoting the prophecy of Isaiah (Luke 4:18–22; Isaiah 61:1–2), and he demonstrated the power of the Spirit in his preaching, in his healing miracles, and in his authority over evil spirits. Peter doubtless echoed the preaching of the New Testament church when he told Cornelius 'how God anointed Jesus of Nazareth with the Holy Spirit and power, and how he went around doing good and healing all who were under the power of the devil, because God was with him' (Acts 10:38).

The Baptist's prophecy was fulfilled on the day of Pentecost. The risen Christ told his disciples to wait: 'Do not leave Jerusalem, but wait for the gift my Father promised, which you have heard me speak about. For John baptised with water, but in a few days you will be baptised with the Holy Spirit' (Acts 1:4–5). A few verses further on the purpose of the gift is announced: 'You will receive power when the Holy Spirit comes upon you, and you will be my witnesses in Jerusalem, and in all Judea and Samaria, and to the ends of the earth' (Acts 1:8).

There is one more reference to being 'baptised with the Holy Spirit' in Acts. It occurs as Peter was explaining to the Church in Jerusalem what had happened at what came to be called 'the Pentecost of the Gentiles':

'As I began to speak, the Holy Spirit came upon them as he had come on us at the beginning. Then I remembered what the Lord had said: "John baptised with water, but you will be baptised with the Holy Spirit." So if God gave them the same gift as he gave us, who believed in the Lord Jesus Christ, who was I to think that I could oppose God?' (Acts 11:15–17)

The only other text in the New Testament which might be regarded as a source of the phrase is in 1 Corinthians 12, where Paul was contrasting the diversity of spiritual gifts in the Church with the unity of Christians:

The body is a unit, though it is made up of many parts; and though all its parts are many, they form one body. So it is with Christ. For we were all baptised by one Spirit into one body – whether Jews or Greeks, slave or free – and we were all given the one Spirit to drink. (1 Corinthians 12:12–13)

The Promise of the Father

These are key texts in the preaching of Pentecostals. They believe all Christians should receive 'the promise of the Father'. In their understanding the appeal of Acts 2:38–9 is normative: 'Repent and be baptised, every one of you, in the name of Jesus Christ for the forgiveness of your sins. And you will receive the gift of the Holy Spirit. The promise is for you and your children and for all who are far off – for all whom the Lord our God will call.' Although the coming of the Spirit on that occasion was not accompanied by the same manifestations of wind and fire, the promise is extended to all generations and peoples who repent and believe in Jesus Christ.

Other verbs are used to describe the Spirit's coming: 'being filled', 'received', 'given', 'anointed with', and 'renewed in': these have all come into the Church's devotions and teaching. In view of the prominence given to 'being baptised in the Holy Spirit' in the New Testament, it is surprising that little was said about it before the revivals of the eighteenth and nineteenth centuries. This neglect is reflected in the use of the titles of Christ in John 1. 'Son of God' and 'Lamb of God' are very common, but 'Baptiser in the Spirit' is unknown outside Pentecostal-charismatic circles.

Probably this is because the early Church assumed that the promise of the Father is fulfilled in water baptism. Claims about receiving the Spirit outside the rites of initiation came from movements for revival and renewal which broke away from the Church. Among the most well-known of these in the early centuries were the Montanists, who claimed extraordinary gifts of the Spirit and rejected water baptism, and the Messalians (from an Aramaic word meaning 'the praying ones'), who taught that every believer must be baptised with fire to dispel the presence of devils and who rejected the need for church structures and sacraments.

Dissident movements such as these – and they occurred in practically every century – caused the Church to insist that the

Spirit worked through her ministries and sacraments, and that extraordinary manifestations of the Spirit must be subject to the authority of her hierarchy.

But not all charismatic movements were divisive. Some were given space within the Church's fellowship to follow their own vision of what the Christian pilgrimage should be. Many religious orders, for example, originated in the charismatic ministries of individuals and groups who collected round them followers to carry on their work after their deaths. Their rules and constitutions were officially recognised by the ecclesiastical authorities, and they formed an international, extra-parochial network within the Church with a good deal of independence from the oversight of local bishops.

Admission to a religious order was sometimes referred to as a 'second baptism'. Bernard of Clairvaux (1090–1153) explained that it was so called because it helped the brothers to be more obedient to Christ: 'It restores the divine image in the soul and makes us Christ-like, much as baptism does.'[1] The concept may have come from an ancient custom of referring to those who were reconciled to the Church after doing penance as receiving a 'second baptism'. Medieval religious orders had a penitential character.

One of the earliest known uses of the phrase, baptism in the Spirit, appeared in the writing of the Orthodox monk, Symeon the New Theologian (949–1022). Symeon became abbot of the monastery of St Mamas in Asia Minor at the age of thirty-one. At that time monasticism, patronised by the Byzantine emperor as a means of maintaining unity within his empire, had become worldly, and monks had lost much of their spirit of poverty, detachment and commitment to prayer.

Symeon in his sermons exhorted his brethren to repentance and conversion of heart, pressing on them the need of a stage in the Christian life which is beyond baptism in water, which he called 'baptism in the Holy Spirit'. This second baptism, he said, gives a deeper awareness of Jesus Christ as Lord and Saviour.

Symeon quoted from the same scriptural texts that Pentecostals use to highlight the need for this Spirit-baptism. He appealed to the example of the early Jerusalem community's sending of Peter and John to Samaria to pray for those who had already been 'baptised in the name of the Lord Jesus' (Acts

8:14ff) that they 'might receive the Holy Spirit, for he had not yet descended on any of them.' This baptism in the Spirit, Symeon said, is accomplished when we cry out in sorrow to be reborn of the Spirit:

> Display a worthy penitence by means of all sorts of deeds and words, that you may draw yourselves to the grace of the all-holy Spirit. For this Spirit when he descends on you becomes like a pool of light to you, which encompasses you completely in an unutterable manner. As it regenerates you, it changes you from corruptible to incorruptible, from mortal to immortal, from sons of men into sons of God, and gods by adoption and grace – that is, if you desire to appear as kinsmen and fellow-heirs of the saints and enter with them into the kingdom of heaven.[2]

Symeon believed, then, that there was a second baptism of the Spirit which led members of the community into greater holiness and to a share in the divine nature of God. Known as the *admirabile commercium*, the 'wonderful exchange', it is expressed in an ancient collect for Christmas:

> Almighty God,
> who wonderfully created us in your own image
> and yet more wonderfully restored us
> through your Son Jesus Christ:
> grant that, as he came to share in our humanity,
> so we may share the life of his divinity;
> who is alive and reigns with you and the Holy Spirit,
> one God, now and for ever.[3]

The Reformers certainly believed in the Christian's need of God's Spirit, but they did not use the phrase. Martin Luther (1483–1546) taught that we are justified by faith and that the Spirit then works in us to bring us to greater obedience and holiness. We may still be prone to disobedience, since we are at the same time justified and sinful (*simul iustus et peccator*), but the Spirit will strengthen us when we repent and turn afresh to Jesus Christ as our Saviour. John Calvin (1509–64) interpreted Paul's renewing of the mind as the real beginning of life, a transformation brought by the Spirit.

The more radical among the English dissidents placed even greater reliance on the enlightening of the Spirit, abandoning outward forms of worship entirely. Isaac Penington (1617–80), who was imprisoned because he would not join in the worship of the established Church, encouraged his fellow Quakers:

> Press your spirit to bow daily before God and wait for breathings to you from his Spirit. . . . Pray that he will give you strength in all the trials which may come your way. By his secret working in your spirit, giving you assistance from time to time, you will advance nearer and nearer towards the kingdom.[4]

Evangelical Revivals

An important figure in the present-day use of the phrase is Jonathan Edwards (1703–58), the American pastor-theologian, who was a key figure in the Great Awakening. The central theme of his preaching and writing was that we need to allow the Spirit to purify and to set on fire our emotions as well as to accept the truth of the gospel with our intellect. The heart as well as the mind must be engaged. In the language of the day, this was 'seriousness' or 'earnestness' in religion or, to quote the title of his most famous work, *Religious Affections*. This surrender of the heart Edwards called the baptism of the Holy Ghost: 'When we receive the Spirit of God, we receive the baptism of the Holy Ghost who is like "fire," and along with it the sanctifying and saving influences of God. When this happens, when grace is at work within us, it sometimes "burns" within us, as it was for Jesus' disciples (Luke 24:32).'[5]

For Edwards the baptism of the Spirit was not specifically to do with power for ministry but an openness of the whole of ourselves to the Spirit for holiness of life. 'That is why it is written that God has given his people the spirit of power, and of love, and of a sound mind (2 Tim 1:7).' He insisted on the importance of discerning what was truly of the Spirit and what was counterfeit, as in his day the Awakening threw up many instances of spurious spiritual claims.

Edwards seems to have been influenced by Zinzendorf and the Moravians who travelled extensively following the 'golden summer' of 1727 at Herrnhut, when the community experienced what one called 'a day of the outpouring of the Holy Spirit', and another said, 'We were baptised by the Holy Spirit himself in one love.'

In England the Methodists responded to this call to holiness. John Wesley (1703–91) met the Moravians during his voyage to America, and he was also an admirer of Edwards' writings. He preached that the Spirit purges the hearts of believers from sin, perfects them in God's love, and thereby empowers them for effective Christian witness. He called this 'entire sanctification'. Once hearts are open to the Spirit, men and women are cleansed from inbred sin that they might be filled with the perfect love of God for true spiritual worship and acceptable service.

Although for Wesley justification must lead to sanctification if believers opened themselves to the Lord, practical experience in ministering to men and women showed him that the remission of sins and the creation of a new heart in the life of a believer were two moments of grace – intimately linked yet separately discernible. He wrote: 'We do not know a single instance in any place of a person's receiving, in one and the same moment, remission of sins, the abiding witness of the Spirit, and a new, a clean heart.'[6]

It was this practical experience, based on Wesley's understanding of the Scriptures, which prepared the way for the doctrine of the 'second blessing' which was to figure prominently in later Holiness and Pentecostal teaching.

As far as it is known, Wesley never used the phrase baptism in the Spirit and never spoke in tongues. But his emphasis on 'the inner witness of the Spirit' to justification and sanctification, giving an assurance of sins forgiven and a heart made clean by the operation of the Spirit, laid the foundations of the Holiness teaching. It was among Wesley's followers, particularly George Whitefield (1714–70), that the phrase came to be used to describe Wesley's teaching on sanctification. Baptism in the Spirit was the doorway leading to a holy life. Whitefield may have learned it from Edwards and his followers during visits to America.

The Holiness Movement

The phrase appeared more frequently in the revivals of the next century. Charles Finney (1792–1876) did more than anyone to popularise it during his missions. He taught that after an individual's conversion there is another experience that a Christian ought to expect: the baptism of the Spirit. Only after we have received that, he said, can we expect to grow in holiness, for such growth is essentially the work of the Spirit in us.

The Holiness movement drew people together in all kinds of groupings from Methodist, Baptist, Congregational and Presbyterian churches. Many new churches with a variety of biblical-sounding names were born. Not least important was the rise of black churches as former slaves found a new identity in American society in the years following the Civil War. It was among these that baptism in the Spirit was often taught. It was also among these that speaking in tongues was experienced – though not apparently at this stage linked with baptism in the Spirit.

Camp-meetings were one of the strategies used to build up Christians in faith and experience. The National Camp-meeting Association for the Promotion of Christian Holiness, formed in New Jersey in 1867 (since 1971 the Christian Holiness Association) emphasised baptism in the Spirit as the means of the believer's crisis experience in sanctification.

Much of this took place in North America, but the revivals influenced Christians in the British Isles. Edward Irving (1792–1834) had preached a baptism in the Spirit and witnessed spiritual gifts being exercised in his Regent Square Church in London. There was an awakening in the sixties resulting in an English camp-meeting which eventually became the Keswick Convention. This gathering in the Lake District had a strong Holiness flavour in its early years.

During the Welsh revival of 1904 Evan Roberts urged people to receive Spirit-baptism. Touring Britain in the same year Richard Torrey preached that baptism in the Spirit is an endowment of God's power not just for ministers but for all Christians for their witness in Jesus' name:

> The baptism of the Holy Spirit is an operation of the Spirit distinct from and subsequent to his regenerating work. A man may be regenerated by the Holy Spirit and still not

baptised by the Spirit. In regeneration there is an impartation of life, and the one who receives it is fitted for service. Every true believer has the Holy Spirit. But not every believer has the baptism with the Holy Spirit, though every believer . . . may have it.[7]

So the Holiness movement provided the concepts and expectations which were to come together in the Pentecostal churches at the turn of the century with dynamic effect. These churches' amazing vigour and growth was due to the fusion of Holiness teaching on baptism in the Spirit with the experience of the charism of speaking in tongues as a sign that God was equipping his people for the living and preaching of the gospel. This was the thrust which eventually made such an impression on members of older denominations.

It was an Anglican who prophesied that it would. F. D. Maurice (1807–72), seeing these developments around him, predicted that the new awareness of the Spirit which he found outside the Church of England would lead to a reformation even deeper and more searching than that of the sixteenth century.

His contemporaries, who had grave misgivings about his orthodoxy, did not believe him.

4

Tongues as Sacrament

What was for me the classic example of a Catholic Anglican experience of baptism in the Holy Spirit happened in 1974. I had been invited to give an address at a conference of Anglican religious at York on the new charismatic communities which were being founded at that time. While I was at the conference I met a friend, Derek Allen, formerly principal of St Stephen's House, Oxford, who asked me to pray for him for renewal in the Spirit.

It was such a busy time that the only chance we had of getting together privately was to skip evensong one day. He came to my room and we recited the office together. Then he said he wanted to make his confession, which he did, kneeling by my chair. I pronounced the absolution, stood up, laid my hands on his head and prayed that he might be baptised in the Spirit. Within a few moments he lifted his hands in the air and began speaking in tongues. Finally, he leapt to his feet and gave me a great hug.

I call it a classic example because in that experience I witnessed the renewal of the baptismal faith (which is what going to confession, or the ministry of reconciliation, really is) and the Pentecostal renewal coming together.

Derek had, I know, been to confession many times before in his life; and he was himself a gifted spiritual director. But at that particular time in his life he was having to face disappointments and difficult decisions (he had not yet been appointed to the parish of St Saviour, Eastbourne, where he was to spend very happily the last years of his life), and the Lord met him – if I may put it crudely – with a new spiritual gift of tongues in a manner which was tailor-made for a priest of his Catholic Anglican tradition!

This charism is so closely identified with Pentecostal teaching and charismatic experience that we must examine it more

closely. In the New Testament *glossolalia* is the normal designation for 'languages'. The manifestation which accompanied
the outpouring of the Spirit on the day of Pentecost in Acts 2
was understood to mean that. Luke believed the apostles had
been given the spontaneous ability to praise God in different
languages, and for him it was a sign that the triumph of Jesus
Christ had overcome the national and linguistic divisions
created by Babel (Genesis 11).

Apart from the reference in Mark 16:17, where the gift of
tongues seems to refer to the same ability, the charism is
nowhere else mentioned in the New Testament except in 1
Corinthians 12–14 where Paul discusses its proper use along
with other 'word gifts' – interpretations of tongues, prophecy,
revelations, instructions. Most biblical scholars do not accept
that in this letter Paul is referring to exactly the same manifestations as in Acts. But Pentecostals have no such hesitations.
For them, all references to tongues in the New Testament are
to one and the same gift.

Modern versions translate the Greek as 'languages', but the
older form, 'tongues', persists among Pentecostals and Charismatics. For convenience I shall use the older form.

The many Pentecostals believe that tongues is a supernatural
gift. Others, including most Charismatics, accept it may well be
a human facility enhanced by the Spirit's anointing for God's
purposes. For those who do not wish to draw too sharp a
distinction between the natural and the supernatural, it is an
instance of how God, besides working miraculously when he
wishes, takes what is natural and endows it with his grace.

Tongues can be natural in the sense that it can be learned.
Social psychologists point out that wordless cries and chants
are a feature of human relationships in all ages and cultures.
Alpine shepherds attract attention by yodelling. In psychologi-
cal jargon it is a preconceptual or transrational mode of communication – that is, conveying thoughts and feelings to others
without using the intelligible words of normal speech.

But whether it is a natural gift enhanced by God's grace or
a supernatural manifestation, Pentecostals and Charismatics are
united in their belief that, when they speak in tongues, the
Spirit guides what they utter so that it becomes a form of
communication with God.

Philologians who have listened to tapes of glossolalia at charismatic meetings report they have not heard known languages. I do not know how thorough their researches have been, but stories continue to circulate about gifts of tongues being recognised as known languages. A friend of mine recently led a party to Israel. On the shores of the Sea of Galilee they prayed together and one of them spoke in tongues. The Israeli guide who was with them told them afterwards that what he had heard was a prayer of praise to God in Hebrew. Since no one had a tape recorder handy, it is impossible to prove that it was.

The bestowal of a gift of tongues when an individual is receiving ministry for baptism in the Spirit is regarded by Pentecostals as the initial evidence that the blessing has been given. This is known as 'evidential tongues'. The teaching is based on the part tongues played among the apostles on the day of Pentecost and also among the Gentiles when they received the Spirit (Acts 10:46 and 19:6).

In his first sermon Peter put into the mouth of Jesus words which were attributed to the Messiah prophetically in Psalm 16:8–11. In that psalm Christ declares that God would not abandon him to the grave: 'Therefore my heart is glad and my tongue rejoices'. Perhaps the gift of tongues among believers was regarded as analogous to the 'glad tongue' of Jesus – a means whereby the Church rejoices in the Spirit as Jesus, the mediator between God and humanity, rejoiced prior to his resurrection.

When they spoke in tongues, then, the members of the apostolic Church had a strong sense of continuity with Jesus, who received the Spirit at his baptism and was raised from death by the Spirit, and of their unity with him. The barriers of religion and race had been broken. Pentecostals expect tongues to play a similar role today.

In this early Pentecostals challenged the dispensational view that the spiritual experiences of Acts were unique and that tongues was a gift (a special 'dispensation' from God) only for the apostolic Church. Such dispensationalism was tacitly accepted by most Anglicans until recently. We have had little experience of glossolalia in our history. We are chary of prophets. And we are neurotically shy of anything that might be the miraculous. It takes a lot for Anglicans to regard speaking in tongues as normative for many Christians!

Tongues Among Anglicans

Many charismatic Anglicans pray in tongues, but they have not followed Pentecostals in expecting all to have the charism (arguing that Paul expected a negative answer when he asked the question, 'Do all speak in tongues?' in 1 Corinthians 12:30). They realise that millions of Christians throughout the ages have entered into the fulness of the Spirit without this particular gift. Nevertheless, Charismatics encourage fellow Christians to be open to receiving it. They know from experience how valuable this gift can be for those on whom God chooses to bestow it.

Glossolalia is used privately as a means of interceding for others and for praying in a contemplative fashion. Used in prayer groups or in church services, and accompanied by a gift of interpretation of tongues, it can sometimes be a powerful means of hearing a prophetic word from the Lord (subject, of course, to testing and discernment).

Also during services, Charismatics can sing in tongues spontaneously, resulting in a beautiful harmony of sound known as 'singing in the Spirit'. These experiences have prompted students of liturgy to look at ancient sources with new eyes and discover references to practices which seem to be related to the glossolalia.

The Fathers knew a form of praise which they called *jubilatio*. Before liturgists became aware of Pentecostal practices, it was assumed that jubilation was spontaneous praise in a known language, using the psalms or other material. Now many of them think that jubilation was akin to 'singing in the Spirit' and that it accompanied the liturgy in the early centuries. Among illiterate peoples it provided a means of expressing joy in the Lord without the benefit (or limitation!) of hymnbooks. So, for example, when a congregation sang the *Alleluia* before the reading of the Gospel (a regular feature of the eucharist in the East and West) the final 'a' could lead into a long wordless song, rather as present-day Charismatics will begin singing in the Spirit at the end of a chorus.

Augustine (354–430) wrote:

He who sings a jubilus does not utter words; he pronounces a wordless sound of joy; the voice of his soul pours forth

happiness as intensely as possible, expressing what he feels
without reflecting on any particular meaning; to manifest his
joy, the man does not use words that can be pronounced and
understood, but he simply lets his joy burst forth without
words; his voice then appears to express a happiness so
intense that he cannot formulate it.[1]

Thomas Aquinas (1225–74) suggested jubilation is the new
song which Christians sing when they are renewed in God's
grace, expressing the mystical and wondrous experience of
Christian discipleship: 'That man truly sings in jubilation who
sings about the good things of glory.'

One of the most famous descriptions of jubilation-filled
worship is in the account of the mass at which Francis of Assisi
was formally canonised by the pope in 1228, two years after his
death. During the first part of the service, the story of Francis'
life and miracles was read. The pope was so moved that he
wept; so did the other clergy and the congregation. Then the
pope lifted up his hands to heaven and proclaimed Francis to
be enrolled among the saints.

At these words the reverend cardinals, together with the
pope, began to sing the *Te Deum* in a loud voice. Then there
was raised a clamour among the many people praising God:
the earth resounded with their mighty voices, the air was
filled with their jubilations, and the ground was moistened
with their tears. New songs were sung, and the servants of
God jubilated in melody of the Spirit. Sweet sounding organs
were heard and spiritual hymns were sung with well-modu-
lated voices. A very sweet odour was breathed, and a most
joyous melody that stirred the emotions resounded there.[2]

References such as these, spanning the centuries, sound very
much like singing in the Spirit. But of course we cannot be
sure. What we do know is that jubilation gradually disappeared
from Christian worship as liturgical celebrations became the
task of choirs and the laity were reduced to a passive role.
Some historians of church music speculate that singing in the
Spirit was the original form of sung liturgical prayer which
eventually produced Gregorian chant – the ancestor of
plainsong.

Some of the medieval mystics prayed in tongues when deep

prayer led into ecstatic cries of joy. Evelyn Underhill commented:

> Acute emotional reactions ... are a normal episode in the early development of many mystics; upon whom the beauty and wonder of the new world of spirit now perceived by them and the Presence that fills it, have often an almost intoxicating effect. Richard Rolle, Ruysbroech, and others have left us vivid descriptions of the jubilus, which seems to have been in their day, like the closely related speaking with tongues in the early Church, a fairly common expression of intense religious excitement.[3]

There are occasional references to glossolalia in Puritan groups after the Reformation. We have already mentioned that it was experienced among those influenced by the Holiness movement of the nineteenth century, culminating in the teaching of the Pentecostals. But it has not been accepted by them uncritically. Watson E. Mills, general secretary of the Pentecostal World Conference, wrote: 'I consider it heresy to speak of speaking in tongues ... clapping, dancing, as manifestations of the Holy Spirit. There are purely human reactions to the power of the Holy Spirit which frequently hinder more than help to bring forth genuine manifestations.'[4]

Glossolalia has been the charism which has alerted many Christians to the possibility that other spiritual gifts in the New Testament might be available today as well – gifts like prophecy, healing and miracles. Tongues has acted as a kind of spiritual booster rocket, lifting them to a greater expectancy and faith in what God can do. Tongues may not be the most important of the charisms (an assertion often made nowadays, though I wonder if any gift of God can be unimportant for those on whom he bestows it); but it has certainly had a catalytic effect in changing attitudes towards other spiritual gifts.

Tongues, Charisms and Sacraments

Certain similarities and differences between the charism of tongues and the sacraments can be noted.

1. In teaching Christians to expect the gift of tongues as an initial, physical evidence of Spirit baptism, Pentecostals were

re-introducing to the Church a charism which had long been lost or neglected. For them it was a sign they were entering into an age in which the apostolic Church's experience of the Spirit was being restored with strengthening fellowship, praise, expectation of the second coming, and spiritual gifts including prophecy, healing, signs and wonders, and evangelism. The promise of God to 'those who are far off' (that is, 'far off' in time as well as distance) was being fulfilled. The 'powers of the age to come' (Hebrews 6:5) were breaking in.

Sacraments, too, are gifts which link us with the apostolic Church. Baptism looks back to the baptism of Jesus and to his death and resurrection; it also points forward to his coming kingdom. The eucharist recalls Christ's Passover as a present reality for our salvation; it is also a foretaste of the eternal banquet in the kingdom of God. It is Christ who presides over the sacraments in his Church just as it is Christ who baptises us with his Spirit and bestows his gifts. Sacraments, then, like tongues, are a sign of continuity with the past and of hope for the future in the purposes of God.

2. Tongues and sacramental liturgies have this in common – they are representative physical acts which transcend rational language and thought. In Pentecostal understanding, tongues are not just an accompaniment of Spirit-baptism; they are integral to it, since believers are surrendering their vocal capacities to God as a sign of their desire that all their faculties be available to the Spirit.

Similarly, sacramental liturgies are representative physical acts in which believers seek to surrender themselves to God. The things of creation and the gestures of the human body are the outward and visible signs of God in Christ active among his people. The language used to accompany these sacramental signs is more than a dogmatic explanation of what is going on (though Anglican liturgy sails close to that reef sometimes). True liturgical prayer needs poetic inspiration as well as biblical truth to point us to the mystery of God's love in and through the sacraments.

3. There is always the danger that the gift of tongues might be formalised and the Spirit quenched through our attempts to secure and guarantee an ongoing experience. The charism has been a means of encouraging many Christians to seek further gifts of the Spirit and to engage in ministries which once they

would never have dreamed of undertaking. Some Charismatics can be over-enthusiastic and insensitive in urging others to seek the charism for its own sake. The danger of manipulation is always lurking in the shadow of attempts to teach and encourage the exercise of spiritual gifts. Believe-it-and-claim-it has been the message among some groups.

But that is also true of sacraments. Christians can be so drilled in a personal rule of life that they attend church and receive the sacraments without being open in their hearts to the grace which God is offering to them. Indiscriminate baptism is one example. The use of the confessional without the intention of amendment of life is another. Roman Catholics have invented a word to describe those whose religious observance consists only of going to mass for communion without allowing the Christian faith to interfere with the way they live: 'over-sacramentalised'.

4. Tongues has a more subtle and subconscious role in the worship of the Church than the formal administration of the sacraments. The celebration of baptism, confirmation, eucharist and the rest are intimately involved with liturgies and offices. Although in an emergency baptism may be administered by anyone (by a lay missionary for a convert in an area where there are no clergy, and by a midwife for a dying baby in a hospital where the chaplain is not available), other sacraments require formal prayers and authorised ministers.

With tongues, however, there is an element of spontaneity and patient waiting for the unexpected. Authorised liturgies and ministers are not necessary. Ecclesiastical control is limited only to ensuring that the exercise of the gift is not abused or divisive within the Christian community. Authentic tongues – like other Pentecostal charisms – cannot be learned. They are *gifts*. They express freedom in the Spirit and what is sometimes called the democratisation of the Christian community – everyone can participate in initiating response to and ministering with the power of God without the benefit of clergy!

Sacraments, on the other hand, have to be ordered and celebrated as the Church directs through its canon laws and episcopal regulations. This means that our theology of the sacraments is focussed on the institutional life of the Church as the embodiment of Jesus Christ. We may tell worshippers that he is the one who presides at the eucharist, baptises the believer, forgives the penitent, and so on. But because the administration of the sacraments is inevitably intertwined with matters of ecclesiastical authority and Church order, we tend to explain them and legislate for them in terms of the institution. First we decide what is valid and what is not, and then claim that our decisions have been guided by the Spirit.

Karl Rahner has characterised manifestations of Pentecostal spirituality as a way of shocking the institutional life of the Church and rightly calling it into question as something of limited and temporal significance.[5] In enthusiastic manifestations of charismatic signs we are reminded again of the ultimate source and goal of institutional life (including sacraments) that is the free and transcendent divine-human encounter.

To conclude, the significance of tongues is that it leads to an empowered witness which inspires faith and liberation in others. Initial evidence is not a sign that 'we have the Spirit'; rather, it is – or should be – a sign that the Spirit 'has us' as participants in the work of the kingdom.

It helps us to grasp how Pentecostals maintain both initial evidence and freedom of the Spirit if we realise that tongues functions for them much more as a sacramental sign than as a rationalist guarantee of the Spirit. It's an outward and *audible* sign of inward and spiritual graces: what Walter Hollenweger has called 'an acoustic sacrament'.

However, recent trends in theology are moving away from an institution-focussed understanding of the sacraments to one which interprets the divine presence in the sacraments as dynamic, free and open. This sees the sacraments as encounters with Christ in a way which is closer to our understanding of spiritual gifts.

This is what we must discuss next.

5

Signs and Sacraments

The origins of the sacraments are in the religious practices of the ancient world into which the apostolic Church was born. That world was familiar with sacred signs. The Roman Empire had its shrines and temples. Households had their gods. Incense was burnt before the effigies of the emperor. The so-called 'mystery religions' were popular with their secret rites. Israel had its Scriptures, temple, priesthood and sacrifices (until 70 AD), circumcision, and celebrations with processions and meals on occasions such as Passover, Pentecost and Ingathering. These were regarded as doors through which the people could approach God, hear him and respond to him.

From the Gospels we know that Jesus submitted to the baptism of John. He laid hands on people for blessing and healing. On three occasions he used spittle in curing blindness and dumbness, and he sent a blind man to wash in order to recover his sight. For one woman a healing gift came through the touch of his garments. On the night of his betrayal he celebrated a Passover supper with his disciples, using the customary Jewish prayers but identifying the bread and the wine with his body and blood. After his resurrection he celebrated other meals with them. Then he commissioned them to preach the gospel, to make disciples and to baptise.

We also know Christ's acts were accompanied by words spoken with power. When he preached the gospel, healed the sick, and liberated those possessed by evil spirits, people were conscious that God was at work through him. The authority of his words was expressed in his actions and the results which followed – healing, deliverance, resurrection from death to life. It was the combination of acts and words which, centuries later, were to be identified in theology as the 'form' and the 'matter' of the sacraments (see Appendix 1).

But there is no evidence that he instituted a set of rituals.

He simply commanded his disciples to baptise, to announce the
forgiveness of sins, and to break bread. And that is what they
did. Luke records in Acts how, after the gift of the Spirit at
Pentecost, the apostles and other leaders shared a special meal,
reading the Scriptures and praying together. They baptised new
converts and laid their hands on them. They anointed and laid
hands on the sick and they disciplined sinners. After prayer for
guidance, they appointed new leaders with the laying on of
hands. The picture we are given is of an infant Church guided
and empowered in its activities – rituals as well as prayers and
preaching – by the Spirit.

Gradually a distinctively Christian set of sacred signs evolved.
Believers began to recognise these rituals as means through
which they could reach out to God and he to them. They held
it was only through the risen and reigning Christ they could
approach the Father, and they refused to participate in non-
Christian ceremonies. Some were martyred for their stand.

There was at first no formulated doctrine about how these
Christian rituals acted as ways through to God. Teaching about
them was introduced by the New Testament authors only inci-
dentally, leaving us with basic principles rather than doctrinal
formularies. It was left to later generations of Christians, and
especially to the Fathers, to debate and to teach what the
Church believed she was doing when she ministered her sacred
signs.

The first step was to find a vocabulary. The New Testament
uses the Greek *mysterion*, perhaps borrowed from the mystery
religions, to describe what God has revealed to us through Jesus
Christ. That word was favoured by Paul as he taught about
the incarnation ('the mystery of godliness', 1 Timothy 3:16), the
sacrifice and death of Christ (1 Corinthians 2:1,7), the purpose
of God in summing up all things in Christ ('he made known to
us the mystery of his will', Ephesians 1:9), the transformation
which will take place at the resurrection ('Listen, I tell you a
mystery', 1 Corinthians 15:51), and the plan of God by which
both Jew and Gentile will through his mercy be included in his
kingdom (Romans 11:25).

But the Fathers realised that Christianity included other mysteries as well – the mystery of how sins are forgiven and how
the Holy Spirit is received in baptism, the mystery of how
the risen Christ is present in his Church, especially when in

obedience to his command its members share in the bread and wine of the eucharist. They began to call these rituals 'mysteries', too.

It was Tertullian, writing about the year 210 AD, who, looking round for an equivalent of *mysterion* for his Latin-speaking audience, adopted *sacramentum*. In a discussion of the meaning of baptism, he explained that it was a *sacramentum* because it was similar to the *sacramentum* (oath) which was administered to Roman recruits when they entered the army. The recruit's oath was a religious initiation. It marked the beginning of a new way of life, and it included an oath of allegiance to the emperor. These things were analogous to baptism, said Tertullian, for then the Christian soldier made an oath of allegiance to Jesus Christ and entered a new way of life.

Thus it was that the word 'sacrament' came into use to describe initiation into the Church, which at that time included baptism, anointings, the laying on of hands, and Communion. By extension it became a general term for Christian religious rituals and everything connected with them such as water, oil, blessings, the Scriptures, the feasts of Easter and Pentecost, and so on.

It was not until the era of the medieval Schoolmen, of whom Aquinas was the greatest, that the seven sacraments were defined – baptism, confirmation, eucharist, ordination, reconciliation (then called penance), marriage and anointing of the sick, with their 'matter' (the things or gestures used) and their 'form' (the words spoken to accompany the ritual acts). By then, too, their administration was being controlled by an ever-growing corpus of canon law and liturgical directions.

Another important word was 'grace'. The Greek *charis* was used in the New Testament in a variety of ways, but it had a special significance in denoting God's favour, forgiveness, and loving-kindness, especially in the sending of his Son. As the Church's theology of the sacraments developed, 'grace' came to be used increasingly of what it was that God gave to his people through the sacraments.

When they took part in the rituals, Christians thought of themselves as receiving 'the grace of the sacraments' or 'sacramental grace'. Because the New Testament states that it is only by means of God's grace that we are saved, the sacraments were seen as vital to salvation. In fact, grace became so closely associated with the sacraments that its use in other contexts tended to be neglected before the Reformation.

Sacramental Efficacy

Having now identified these rituals as sacraments, it became necessary to explain how and why God's grace could be received through them. For these theological explanations the Fathers relied on the Bible, on their own experience of the sacramental rituals, and on what their predecessors and contemporaries said about them.

If the Scriptures say that baptism forgives sins, the Fathers concluded, then that must be so. If at the last supper Jesus said, 'This is my body', then the eucharist bread must be his body. And if by laying their hands on people the apostles conferred the gift of the Holy Spirit, then, when their successors did the same, the Spirit must be conferred also. For the Scriptures were read as the Word of God, and what God said must be true. The Fathers expounded these themes in their sermons and writings with a wealth of scriptural exposition, imagery and allegory.

Their theological conclusions were confirmed in their experience of the sacraments. They knew in their own lives, and from observing the lives of others, that baptism often did result in a new and more Christlike way of living. They knew that at the eucharist they and others became aware they were eating and drinking in the Lord's presence. They knew that those on whom they laid hands for ecclesiastical appointments often became good pastors and missioners. They therefore taught that when sacramental signs were performed, God's grace came to those who received them, provided they accepted these signs with repentance and faith. The foundations were laid for the traditional understanding of the sacraments as outward and visible signs of inward and spiritual grace.

What forced them to define the sacraments further was the rise of heresies and the effects of persecution. These events faced them with awkward questions. How were they to regard baptism which had been carried out by heretical bishops and priests who, say, denied the divinity of Christ? Were the eucharists presided over by clergy who had lapsed in the face of persecution authentic celebrations of the Lord's Supper? Did these men lose the gift of the Spirit when they fell into error or apostasised? Could they still minister the sacraments and be channels of God's grace?

In wrestling with these questions, the Fathers came to believe that the sacraments were effective in themselves because it was Christ who works through them and his sovereignty overrules the sinfulness of humanity. Sacraments were signs of the new covenant which he had won on the cross. And just as that new covenant with its promise of salvation was effective whether or not individuals responded to it so, too, the sacraments were effective means of offering his saving grace to us irrespective of the worthiness of the minister or the weakness of our faith.

In this way the concept of sacramental efficacy entered the Church's teaching. This meant that when a sacrament like baptism is performed with the pouring of water and the recital of the traditional words by one authorised by the Church to preside over it, then God's forgiveness and adoption come through the sacramental sign irrespective of the disposition of the minister and that of the catechumen. The sacred sign had become a sure channel of God's grace. In later centuries this teaching about sacramental efficacy came to be known as *ex opere operato*, 'from the doing of the thing done' – a teaching which was to be misunderstood as conferring a magic power to the sacraments.

Of course, sacramental efficacy does not mean that sacraments automatically benefit either the minister or the recipient. The minister who presides over the sacraments carelessly or unfaithfully is acting unworthily. Those who receive the sacramental signs without repentance and faith are guilty of dishonouring the Lord. The Fathers had no intention of ignoring the New Testament's teaching on the relationship between grace, repentance and faith. They knew Paul was severe in his condemnation of those who went to Communion without repenting their sins: 'Anyone who eats and drinks without recognising the body of the Lord eats and drinks judgment on himself' (1 Corinthians 11:29). But they were convinced that the divine initiative which had sent Jesus into the world for our salvation was also present in the sacramental signs of that salvation. Grace is there for us to receive it, and if we are repentant and faithful, then it is fruitful in our lives.

Sacramental Character

The other teaching which emerged relevant to our discussion is that of the sacramental seal or, as it is more often called, 'sacramental character'. Here again the Scriptures, tradition and experience all played their part in formulating the doctrine. It was the Fathers' attempt to answer the question, what did Paul mean when he said that Christians are 'sealed with the Spirit'? (Ephesians 1:13–14, 4:30)

In those days, as now, a seal was a stamp, or the mark it made, to denote ownership. The New Testament authors extended this literal meaning into a poetic metaphor to signify that something comes from or belongs to God, like the scroll in the book of Revelation, or the mark on the foreheads of those who are to be spared the final tribulation (Revelation 5:1, 7:2–4). The fourth Gospel affirms that God set his seal on his Messiah, making him his Son (John 6:27, 10:36). Paul said God has put his seal on Christ's followers as a foretaste of things yet to come (2 Corinthians 1:22). In the apostle's understanding, being sealed with the Spirit seems to be a metaphorical way of speaking about the experience of being filled with the Spirit.

Many early Christians felt inwardly changed, as if they had been 'touched' or 'stamped' by God himself. Those who knew them noticed that their lives were transformed. Therefore the Fathers concluded that these texts were more than metaphorical. Taking the Johannine passages literally, the seal becomes a reality which marks Christians off from others.

But what kind of reality was it? What exactly was this seal? Searching the Scriptures further, they noted those passages which spoke about anointing, since in some being anointed with the Spirit seemed to be another way of referring to being sealed with the Spirit. Furthermore, since a physical seal left its visible impression or image, so also, it was argued, those who were sealed with the Spirit were made in the 'image of God'.

Paul wrote, 'He [God] anointed us, set his seal of ownership on us, and put his Spirit in our hearts as a deposit, guaranteeing what is to come' (2 Corinthians 1:21–2). John, too, speaks of receiving the Spirit in terms of an anointing: he reminds his readers that they have been anointed with the Holy One, and that this anointing remains with them, revealing the truth to them (1 John 2:20, 27). Since Jesus was anointed by the Spirit at his baptism as Messiah (Luke 3:21–2; 4:18–25; Acts 4:27), weren't Christians also anointed into his Messiahship at their baptism?

On these texts, therefore, the Fathers taught that those who receive the seal of the Spirit are changed into a new likeness of God by becoming conformed to the image of his Son (Romans 8:29; 2 Corinthians 3:18). They put on Christ, or put on a nature which is being renewed in the image of God (Galatians 3:27; Colossians 3:10). They become radically different from other people. God's seal on Christ made him his Son, and those who look at Christ see the image of the Father. Similarly, Christ's seal on his disciples makes them sons and daughters of God, for they all bear the stamp of their Father, the Spirit's seal.

Applied to baptism, then, the biblical metaphor became an invisible or metaphysical reality. The sacrament was now regarded as a sign that God was sealing you as his own. Nothing could take it away from you. And since it was the practice from New Testament times only to baptise once, it was assumed that the sealing was permanent.

Some Fathers thought that it was through the water of baptism that the Spirit marked you, others that it was through the anointing with oil, which was introduced to the rites of initiation at an early stage. But whatever you did, even if you sinned, you were still 'branded' – though, of course, you could only be saved if you repented of your sins and were restored to faith. Cyril prayed for the catechumens, 'May God fill you with heavenly treasures of the new covenant and sign you with that seal of the Holy Spirit that no man shall break for ever.'

The same concept of a sacramental seal was applied to those who were ordained. Once you became a deacon, a presbyter or a bishop, you were not ordained again. That remained the practice even if you fell into heresy or apostasised in the face of persecution. If you repented, you were disciplined and for a period of time barred from Communion. Then hands were laid on you as a sign of reconciliation to God and to the Church through Christ. But you were not baptised (or ordained) again. The sacramental character remained, though what that means in terms of an individual's final salvation only God can judge.

The story of the development of the sacraments from this sketch of their scriptural and patristic beginnings is a long and complicated one. It would take us through the history of the Church up to the great division between East and West in the eleventh century, through the scholastic controversies of the Middle Ages which led to the definition of the seven sacraments, through the blessings and abuses associated with the sacraments up to the Reformation, the fragmentation of the Western Church in the sixteenth and seventeenth centuries and the consequent controversies about sacramental teaching and practice.

During this time Christian teachers often found themselves going beyond the descriptions and interpretations they found in the New Testament putting forward more philosophical explanations of the Church's sacramental practices. Many of these speculations have been found wanting by later generations (e.g., transubstantiation). But some have found a more permanent place in the Church's sacramental theology. They were philosophical theories which pulled together revelation and experience, belief and practice, into a coherent pattern for different generations.

Belief in – or, at any rate, a tacit acceptance of – sacramental efficacy and sacramental character in some form or other has survived in almost all Christian denominations. The doctrines give us the assurance that, provided we have the desire to repent and to be faithful, the sacraments are a covenanted means by which we are offered God's grace irrespective of our feelings and whether or not the minister is worthy.

What is striking is how much the traditional doctrines of sacramental efficacy and sacramental character rely on the same biblical texts which Pentecostals and Charismatics use in teaching about the work of the Holy Spirit. Yet these same doctrines have created a big difference between our understanding of sacraments and of spiritual gifts. And the consequences of that difference have been far-reaching in the pastoral life of the Church, and especially in the effect of the charismatic renewal today.[1]

6

The Spirit and the Sacraments

Out of the Reformation controversies about sacramental teaching and practice, the Tudor and Stuart Anglicans created the Book of Common Prayer, the ordinal and the Thirty-Nine Articles. The theology undergirding these formularies reflects a mixture of reformed Catholicism and continental Protestantism which was the outcome of the upheavals in England, from 1532 when Henry VIII and Parliament began the breach with Rome, to 1662 when the book took its final shape. That theology included the acceptance of sacramental efficacy and sacramental character, but was purged of what were considered the unbiblical abuses and medieval accretions associated with these concepts.

Baptism and the eucharist were distinguished as 'sacraments of the gospel' since only they had been instituted, so it was believed, by Jesus Christ himself. Provision was made in the Prayer Book for the administration of four out of the other five 'commonly called sacraments' – confirmation, marriage, ordination, and reconciliation. A service of Communion for the sick was included, but no form for anointing with the laying on of hands. That was rejected because the Anglican Reformers could see no scriptural justification for the form in which it was administered in their times – as an extreme unction for the dying. 'Where is our command to regard chrism as a sacrament?' Martin Bucer had asked Thomas Cranmer, when invited to comment on the 1549 Prayer Book; and unction was dropped in the revision of 1552.[1]

Infant baptism was the norm, a rite for adults being added in the 1662 Prayer Book, 'for the baptising of natives in our plantations, and others converted to the faith.' Confirmation was administered by a bishop when the baptised were old enough to learn the Catechism. The Articles rejected doctrines of 'sacrifices of masses' and transubstantiation and declared:

'The body of Christ is given, taken, and eaten, in the Supper,
only after an heavenly and spiritual manner. And the mean
whereby the body of Christ is received and eaten in the Supper
is faith.' The thanksgiving prayer referred only to 'sacrifice of
praise and thanksgiving'.

However, in the 1662 rite the sacrament was given to communicants with the words, 'The Body of our Lord Jesus Christ
which was given for thee' and, 'The Blood of our Lord Jesus
Christ which was shed for thee', and the rubrics directed that
what remained of the consecrated bread and wine were to be
consumed reverently, suggesting at least a reverence for the
sacrament as a sign of Christ's presence. The Prayer Book
assumed that all who attended the service would receive the
bread and the wine. Communicants were expected to be confirmed or 'desirous to be confirmed'. The only barrier was grave
sin.

Within the wide boundaries of these formularies later generations of Anglican scholars advanced a variety of interpretations of the sacraments, especially in relation to the eucharist.
In what sense could the Lord's Supper be called the Christian
sacrifice? In what sense could it be said that Christ was present
in the consecrated elements? There were disagreements about
the scriptural authority for confirmation and reconciliation as
they were taught and practised in certain high church parishes.

These debates sharpened when Catholic Anglicans pressed
for the restoration of a fuller sacramental life to the Church of
England at the end of the nineteenth and the beginning of the
twentieth centuries. But by the second half of the century,
the biblical, liturgical and ecumenical movements were leading the Church of England to review its teaching and practice.
As the denominations worldwide began to discover a convergence of their doctrines of the sacraments, so Evangelical and
Catholic Anglicans began to discern a domestic convergence
among themselves. One of the results of this worldwide process
was the publication of the World Council of Churches' Faith
and Order document No. 111, *Baptism, Eucharist and Ministry*
in 1982 and the replies of the denominations round the world
to it.

Theologians were exploring other ways of understanding the
sacraments besides those which had been handed down to them
from medieval and Reformation times. The pace-setters in this

exploration were the Roman Catholic scholars like Yves Congar, Emil Mersch, Pierre Bouyer and Karl Rahner. Their writings were translated into English and widely read by those who were responsible for the teaching of sacramental theology and the revision of the Church of England's sacramental rites. Particularly influential was the magazine, *La Maison-Dieu*, which in the post-war years was the voice of the mission-conscious French Roman Church and which did much to prepare the way for the liturgical reforms of the Second Vatican Council.

Encounters with Jesus

Catholic Anglicans, who were used to learning their sacramental theology and liturgical practice from continental Catholicism, absorbed these lessons – though not without a sense of disorientation, for it sometimes seemed as if the Roman Church was veering in an Evangelical direction!

One development was to see the sacraments more as signs of Jesus acting within his body rather than as ritual acts instituted by him and the apostles in the past. The main thrust of this teaching was that what God offers us through the sacraments comes through, with and in Christ by the power of the Holy Spirit. In celebrating the sacraments, then, we who are members of the Church act in union with the same Jesus who once offered himself to the Father as a sacrifice for our sins, and who now reigns with the Father in glory. The sanctifying action of God is made real in the sacraments through Christ by the power of his Spirit.

From this theologians began to reinterpret the sacraments as outward and visible forms of our encounter with the Lord. Traditionally, as we have seen, the sacraments had been thought of as 'channels of God's grace'. Although 'grace' is a good biblical word, in the half-instructed Christian mind it tended to be interpreted in the sense of divine yet somewhat impersonal power flowing through the sacred signs to the recipients. There was an understandable yet subchristian assumption, especially in Catholic Anglican circles, that if I made my confession or my Communion sacramental grace was my holy reward (note the predominance of the personal pronoun in that sentence).

While it is true we need to recognise that God's grace can

energise us for his purposes through the sacraments, this is because through them we don't just receive something but meet Someone – the God who loves us and comes to us where we are. By teaching that in the sacraments there is an encounter between ourselves and Jesus Christ, grace itself can be understood more accurately in terms of growing into a closer relationship with him.

So sacraments are now seen from a different perspective. Instead of beginning with the Scriptures and trying to demonstrate how the sacraments were instituted in the New Testament and handed on in the Church's history, theologians these days begin by recognising that Christ is the Sacrament *par excellence*, manifesting God's love to the world. As he is in his body the Church by his Spirit, so his love is revealed by the Spirit in and through the words, gestures and created things which the Church has discerned as sacred signs. Sacraments are one of the ways in which the message of the gospel is proclaimed and being brought to its fulfilment.

Individually they are occasions when we encounter Christ at particular moments in our earthly pilgrimage – admission to the Christian community, ongoing fellowship, taking a life partner, and so on. The sacraments are rites of passage in the sense that they signify that Jesus is with us at every step we take as we 'pass over' with him in his Passover from this world into the place he has prepared for us.

This sacramental theology relies heavily on a renewed understanding of the operation of the Spirit in and through the sacramental signs. It also underlines the truth that it is within the fellowship of the Spirit that Christ is manifested among us sacramentally. As this understanding percolated through the Church of England and found expression in the revision of the liturgy in Series Two and in Series Three and then in the ASB, the way was being prepared for its members to receive what would be for many new experiences of the Spirit through the charismatic renewal.

Tom Smail was one of the first Anglicans to examine the renewal theologically. He often warns us about being so fascinated with the spiritual gifts that we neglect the Giver. In *The Giving Gift* (1988) he urges us to look beyond the spiritual gifts to God as the Giver of himself, giving himself to us in Christ and giving us to Christ through the Spirit in us:

The Christ who breathes the Spirit upon us now is simul-
taneously, completely and eternally the incarnate, regener-
ated, anointed and glorified Son. The Spirit, whom we receive
from him, is the Spirit who has perfected all his work in
Christ's humanity and, on that basis, can do his work in us
in whatever order and way his love for us directs. (p. 107)

We might add that in the same way, through the Spirit, God
gives himself to us in Christ through the sacramental signs and
we, through the same Spirit, offer ourselves back to him in
Christ. For we are not passive recipients of the sacraments: we
have to respond to them in lives of daily discipleship.

With this comes a new appreciation of the Word of God and
of the manifestations of spiritual gifts in Christians of other
traditions. In a remarkable manner, therefore, the renewal did
much to popularise (that is, make available for wider
understanding) what the biblical, liturgical and ecumenical
movements had been doing for church leaders, theologians,
liturgists and ecumenists in the previous decades.

It also renewed in many the realisation of how necessary
repentance and personal faith are for those who receive the
sacraments, particularly the eucharist. The coming of the Spirit
both convicts us of sin and strengthens our faith. The expectation of encountering Jesus in the sacramental signs can stir
us up to a greater awareness of our need to be obedient to
him. This approach to the eucharist is not far removed from
the old Evangelical dictum that 'All who love the Lord Jesus
are welcome at his Table.' In a later chapter I shall discuss
further the way in which the charismatic renewal has helped
Catholic Anglicans and Evangelicals to draw closer together in
their understanding of the sacrificial significance of the eucharist
and the nature of Christ's presence in the consecrated bread
and wine.

Sacraments as Symbols

Another interpretation of the sacraments is that of symbolism.
Studies of the place of symbolism in human life have revealed
a number of matters which are relevant to our discussion. It has
been shown, for example, that the double meaning of symbolic

actions, and the interaction of one meaning on another, affect participants on many levels.

We only have to think of the significance of, say, a handshake to realise that words like, 'Nice to see you', communicate more when accompanied by this physical gesture than if we simply uttered the words without touching the one we have met. Similarly, inviting a friend – especially a boyfriend or girlfriend – home for a meal to meet the rest of the family can be a highly significant moment for all concerned: the meal and the conversation over the table symbolise a step in a strengthening relationship which would not be so evident if the friend only called in for a brief chat. Sending a Christmas card, giving a birthday present, bringing a bunch of flowers – human relationships are full of symbols which reinforce the meaning of our words, or which sometimes convey thoughts and feelings for which we feel words are inadequate.

This function of symbols has obvious associations with the use of water, the consuming of bread and wine, and the touch of oil and hands. Sacramental signs can be seen as human symbols of communication which have been transfigured (some would say 'tran-sign-ified') by the Spirit into means through which we encounter Christ. There is a parallel here with the way in which natural abilities are also transfigured by the Spirit into spiritual gifts and become manifestations of Christ's power.

Once upon a time, to speak of a sacrament as a symbol was to suggest that it was unreal. That is no longer the case. A symbol is now recognised as having a mysterious reality of its own which lies beneath what is observed, touched, heard or tasted. In the sacraments God reveals and grants salvation through Christ's redeeming work which culminated in his death, resurrection and ascension into heaven; at the same time, the Church worships God through Christ by an active sharing in speech and symbolic actions which are empowered by the Holy Spirit. As the Spirit energised all that Jesus said and did in the days of his flesh, so the Spirit energises all that the body of Christ says and does provided it acts in union with its Head.

So again, in this understanding of the sacraments the role of the Holy Spirit is central. This is reflected in the texts of the new prayers in our revised liturgies for baptism, confirmation, the eucharist and the other sacraments. The Bible, the history of the liturgy, contacts with other denominations (especially

Eastern Orthodox Churches, whose liturgies have never lost a strong pneumatological character) all contribute to this enrichment.

That great symbol of God's Word, the Bible, has acquired a sacramental significance through our awareness of its authority when it is used in worship. The Church of England has always given a high priority to the reading and exposition of the Bible in church services, but in practice the link between preaching and the administration of the sacraments has been weak.

The liturgical movement has restored the interdependence of the ministry of the Word and the ministry of the Sacrament. The revised rites of the ASB with the calendar and lectionary enable us to listen again to God's Word through the Scriptures. In doing this we enter into a long and rich tradition created by the Spirit through the labours of apostles, prophets, evangelists, pastors and teachers, as they proclaimed the gospel of the kingdom and built up the Body of Christ. Modern biblical scholarship contributes to that proclamation. The exegetes help us to grasp more clearly the historical and human beginnings of the Bible. The theologians assist us to understand how God's revelation has unfolded through generations of Christian teaching.

But in the liturgical celebration we have come to expect something fresh as well – God's word to us now, brought out of the readings and the exposition (in whatever form that takes) by the Spirit, who gives us ears to hear. The rites for baptism, confirmation, the eucharist and so on, are designed to enable us to meet Christ in Word and Sacrament, not as separate movements of the Spirit but as responses to sacramental signs of different kinds. Manifestations of charismatic word-gifts (simple prophecies, words of wisdom and knowledge, an interpretation of tongues, or an inspired, spontaneous song) can all add to our awareness of the ministry of the Word and that part of the service where we hope to hear the voice of the Lord.

In the traditional form of the sung eucharist, when the celebrant is assisted by a deacon and sub-deacon, the task of reading or intoning the Gospel passage in the service is given to the deacon. During the singing between the epistle and the Gospel, the deacon takes the book of the Gospels and, before going to the place where he usually reads it, he kneels before the celebrant and asks for a blessing. The celebrant makes the sign of the cross over him and says, 'May the Lord be in your heart and on your lips that you may worthily and fitfully proclaim his Gospel.' That prayer is nothing less than an invocation of the Spirit on the deacon and on the sacramental sign which he is about to perform.

Much that I learned from the charismatic renewal was relevant when I applied its lessons to presiding at worship, preaching, administering the sacraments, and encouraging the development of an every-member-ministry among Christians. Like many other Anglicans, I discovered that the ASB and other supplementary materials published by the Liturgical Commission since have been 'graced' vehicles for sacramental worship leading to ministry and mission.

Again, the close parallels between the sacraments and spiritual gifts are striking.

1. Both are acts of God through Christ among his people. We believe that sacraments and spiritual gifts are revealed in the Scriptures. Christ's ministry can be interpreted both as foreshadowing the use of sacramental signs and also as a demonstration of spiritual gifts. If Christ is the Sacrament *par excellence* he is also the Charismatic *par excellence*. His ministry of teaching, prophecy, knowledge, wisdom, healing, deliverance and martyrdom, culminating on the cross, was charismatic-sacramental.

2. Both sacraments and spiritual gifts equip the body of Christ. The Spirit activates the sacramental signs so that we are assured of Christ's presence in forgiving our sins, bringing his healing, restoring us to fellowship with himself and with one another, and strengthening us for service in his name as pilgrims, ministers, and married couples. The Spirit is also active when he bestows his gifts for the situations of service and evangelism in which he may lead us. In both cases faith is the means through which we respond. In both cases God offers us his means whereby we may grow in holiness and be energised for witness.

3. Spiritual gifts are needed for so many aspects of ministering the sacraments – gifts for leading worship and preaching, gifts for reading the Scriptures and singing the liturgy and the hymns and songs which accompany it, gifts of repentance and faith in preparation for meeting Jesus in and through the sacramental signs, gifts of prayer and praise.

The real difference is that sacraments are covenanted means of grace whereas when spiritual gifts are manifested, the grace has to be discerned in them, which may take time. A gift of healing might be immediate if it is miraculous, but a gift of simple prophecy may not be recognised as authentic until years afterwards, when the recipient can look back and realise how God spoke to him or her through that.

But, having said that, it is also true that the grace of the sacraments is not always immediately evident, either. Sacraments are unfruitful in the lives of unworthy recipients. A man or woman may be ordained a priest, but their lifestyle and attitudes may be a denial of Christ's law of love. When we look at sacraments and spiritual gifts from this angle, the difference between them almost disappears.

7

Water and the Spirit

After being baptised in the Spirit, it is not unusual for some Anglican Charismatics to ask their vicar if they can be baptised in water, usually by immersion. Because the Church of England believes that baptism can only be administered once, for the theological reasons I have explained, the vicar has to refuse.

This can create pastoral problems. For the Charismatic, it seems the Church of England is denying the validity of their experience. Jesus has become real to them in a new way; baptism seems the proper scriptural response (especially if they were christened as infants of non-church parents); explanations about sacramental efficacy and sacramental character are mumbo-jumbo to them. So they go to a Baptist or a New Church for the ceremony – and sometimes join it permanently. For the vicar, it may mean losing another committed Christian from the congregation. And all in the cause of a sacramental theology which took centuries to evolve and which seems to have little relevance to what Charismatics are experiencing now.

This dilemma has been one of the factors in causing a small number of Anglican priests to leave the Church of England. A friend of mine who is ordained felt that he should rebaptise those who came to him in these circumstances, and he went to discuss the matter with his diocesan bishop. Regretfully the bishop told him that if he proceeded with the rebaptisms, he should resign. Being an honourable soul, that is what my friend did. He commented later he was puzzled why the Church of England should expect him to resign for such a reason (and be prepared to lose enthusiastic lay members) when it tolerated much more damaging views and actions by its clergy.

We have seen that in Pentecostal teaching baptism in the Spirit is distinct from water-baptism. Spirit-baptism is not about repentance, faith and membership of the Church; it is about being empowered and gifted for witness and mission. This dis-

tinction is not always understood by Charismatics, who sometimes regard it as a conversion to be followed by water-baptism.

In the early days of the renewal, Charismatics did not have
much opportunity to reflect theologically on what was happening. Some of them used *Saints Alive!* in preparing candidates
for confirmation, with some success, and wondered if confirmation was the equivalent of the Pentecostal experience. Others
imported Pentecostal teaching on a 'second blessing'. Hardly
any Anglican theologians realised the importance of the movement and so could not help them.

Things were different in the Roman Church. A number of
their theologians have either been actively involved in the
renewal, like Heribert Mülhen, Edward O'Connor, Donald
Gelpi and Francis Sullivan, or taken a sympathetic interest in
it, like Yves Congar and Karl Rahner. Consequently much has
been done to open up a discussion on the relationship between
baptism in the Spirit and Christian initiation from the Catholic
understanding of the sacraments.

Two main lines of interpretation developed. One sees the
experience of baptism in the Spirit as a fuller realisation of
the sacrament of Christian initiation within the individual; the
other regards the experience as a deeply significant response
to God at a critical moment in an individual's life, with no
immediate connection with baptism and confirmation.

Spirit-baptism and Initiation

Interpreting baptism in the Spirit as a fuller realisation of
Christian initiation rests on the close connection between water
baptism and the gift of the Spirit in the New Testament, the
use of the phrase, 'be baptised in the Holy Spirit' (Mark 1:8
and parallel passages), the outline of what Christian initiation
entails in passages such as Acts 2:38, 8:17, 10:47, 19:5-6, and
the teaching that both liberation from sin and inner strengthening are works of the Spirit within the believer (Romans 8:18ff.,
etc.).

It also looks to the baptism of Christ as a model or paradigm
of what Christian baptism is to be: just as Jesus was anointed
with the Spirit for his charismatic ministry as he came up out

of the Jordan, so should his disciples similarly be anointed by
the Spirit for their ministries in his name at their baptism.

Charismatic leaders who take this position explain that, when
we were baptised, we received from God a 'Spirit-package'
which included forgiveness for our sins through the cross of
Jesus Christ, adoption as sons and daughters of our heavenly
Father, incorporation into the fellowship of the Spirit, a foretaste of the kingdom of heaven, and a vocation to serve the
Lord for the rest of our lives.

But this 'package' contains so many good things that it takes
the rest of our lives to receive it (or to unpack it, as it is
explained in sermons). What we call baptism in the Spirit,
therefore, is a new release of the Holy Spirit within us, usually
accompanied by a memorable experience of God's love and
perhaps with the bestowal of a new spiritual gift such as tongues.

Because we could not receive all these good things at once,
there is often a time-lag between the administration of the
sacraments (baptism, confirmation and first Communion) and
baptism in the Spirit. It may be years before we come to realise
how much more we need God's equipping than when we first
believed. These leaders point out that this is true for other
things in the 'package' as well. What is involved in the forgiveness of sins and our membership of the body of Christ, for
example, we only comprehend more fully as we grow in spiritual
maturity.

The argument for locating baptism in the Spirit within the
orbit of Christian initiation has been strengthened by the
Roman Catholic scholars Kilian McDonnell and George T.
Montague in their book, *Christian Initiation and Baptism in the
Holy Spirit: Evidence from the First Eight Centuries* (1991).
There they illustrate with texts from the Fathers and the early
baptismal liturgies that the imparting of spiritual gifts was
assumed when catechumens were initiated into the Church. The
newly-baptised were expected to exercise a personal ministry
in the power of the Spirit, notably in prophecy and in prayer.

They go on to show how this expectation was gradually overshadowed by what was perceived as the greater blessing of the
sacrament, namely, the forgiveness of sins and hope of salvation.
In the preaching and celebrating of Christian initiation, the
baptism of Jesus, one of the New Testament paradigms of
initiation, slipped into the background; the other New Testa-

ment paradigm, that of participating in Christ's death and resurrection, came to dominate the Church's teaching (except in the Syrian liturgy which still focussed on Christ's baptism). The Creed unwittingly helped this process because all it declared about baptism was that it was 'for the forgiveness of sins'.

But the most important factor in losing this expectation of spiritual gifts was the practice of infant baptism. In centuries when the rate of infant mortality was high, Christian parents felt their babies should be baptised as soon after birth as possible to ensure their children a place in the kingdom of heaven. This reinforced the belief that the main purpose of baptism was salvation from sin. Augustine taught that infants needed to be washed from the effects of original sin, and his view became universally accepted as an article of faith. Infant baptism also came to be mixed up with folk religion, superstition and social custom, with little real faith in Jesus Christ. The sacrament was thus separated from an expectation of initiation into the Spirit-gifted life of Christian discipleship.

One consequence of the rise of infant baptism was the gradual emergence of confirmation as a separate rite in the Western Church (but not in the Orthodox East). While confirmation never completely lost its connection with baptism, its administration became a formality. In medieval England bishops were few and communications difficult, and children and young people often had to wait years before they were confirmed. The separation of this rite from baptism caused confirmation eventually to acquire the status of an independent sacrament (by the Council of Florence 1439). I shall discuss the relationship between confirmation and baptism in the Spirit in the next chapter.

In *We believe in the Holy Spirit* the Church of England Doctrine Commission opted for the integration of Spirit-baptism with the sacrament of baptism. Among the arguments they put forward is Paul's use of the image of adoption (Romans 8:15; Galatians 4:6): 'Our heavenly Father has, as it were, in baptism signed the necessary legal documents, but as in adoption this marks the beginning of a story' (p. 77).

This interpretation is attractive to sacramentalists. It affirms the objective efficacy of the sacrament. It avoids hints of a 'second baptism'. Because the Spirit works through the sacrament and the experience both 'baptisms' can be understood as aspects of a single encounter with Christ. And it defends the practice of infant baptism, for it relates the promise of the Spirit made in baptism to the believing parents and the community of faith as a whole in the hope that the child will grow into that promise in later years.

But in spite of its attraction, it leaves me feeling uneasy. Are we attempting to domesticate the workings of the Spirit to our sacramental system, itself the result of a long and complicated evolution of ideas and experiences of the Spirit? Is it acceptable to hierarchies because it subjects Spirit-baptism to ecclesiastical control exercised through the administration of the sacraments? Are we afraid that God might, after all, be doing a new thing, upsetting our sacramental theology?

The argument that all the spiritual gifts we could possibly need in life are available in baptism can be stretched beyond credibility. It could, for example, be said that being baptised conveys the charisms for marriage, for ordination, or for being a missionary. Pressed to its logical conclusion, we might ask why is it necessary to receive other sacraments at all if every-thing that we need from the Lord sacramentally is contained in water baptism? Such a position leaves little room for those sovereign acts of God which are oblique to or which challenge the routinised life of the Church and of the individual Christian.

Surprises of the Spirit

For these reasons, the other interpretation is to my mind more persuasive, namely, that baptism in the Spirit is a fresh sending of the Spirit on one who has already received Christ through repentance, faith and water baptism. I recognise that this inter-pretation rests heavily on the pneumatology of Luke and Acts, but that pneumatology is not contradicted by what is revealed of the Holy Spirit's coming in the rest of the New Testament. According to this interpretation, the gift of the Spirit in water baptism admits a believer to the fellowship of the Church; but it is not until later – when the implications of Christian discipleship are beginning to be worked out in his or her life – that the Spirit comes with power.

This interpretation is favoured by many Evangelical Charis-matics. Since they are generally less concerned to relate Spirit-baptism to sacramental teaching, that might be expected. Less expectedly, it is put forward by Francis Sullivan, one of the Roman theologians I have just listed.

Sullivan thinks that his fellow-Catholics are reluctant to speak of a fresh imparting of the Spirit except through the reception of a sacrament because they fear this interpretation would be incompatible with Catholic theology. He sets out to prove otherwise. He writes:

> Perhaps the best way to express my own opinion on this question is to say that I believe that what happens to people in the charismatic renewal is that they are baptised in the Spirit in the *biblical sense* of this term, and that the *biblical sense includes both the theological and the experiential sense.* In other words, in my view, what people are receiving in the charismatic renewal is a real imparting of the Spirit, a new 'outpouring of the Spirit' (the theological sense), which typically has effects that make them aware that the Spirit is working in a new way in their lives (the experiential sense).[1]

Sullivan points out that Aquinas wrestled with the problem of the sending of the Spirit to a place or a person where it may be assumed he is already present. Aquinas came to the conclusion that the sending of the Spirit is not a matter of movement but a matter of presence – or, rather, the degree of presence. The 'coming' of the Spirit is our realisation of a new relationship between ourselves and the Spirit, and this involves a new relationship between God and the Christian.

The examples which the 'angelic doctor' gives – miracles, prophecy, martyrdom – show that he was not thinking within Spirit-baptism categories. These new relationships with the Spirit are related to the manifestation of spiritual gifts in the life of the believer. But it means more than that. Sullivan tells us Aquinas was also thinking of a new way of the Spirit's indwelling within us, and this means an innovation of our relationship with the divine. It means a more intimate and experiential knowledge of God as present within, a knowledge which leads to a more ardent love for him on our part.

Aquinas' discernment of new 'sendings of the Spirit' – or what we might call new 'baptisms in the Spirit' – have been happening to Christian people in every age. In the life-stories of many faithful Christians, there are usually one or more turning-points, conversions, experiences of guidance or power, which have marked a decisive change in that believer's life. Such moments have often been followed by new illuminations of God's purposes, new experiences of God's grace, and new responses to God's love. Sometimes they have been accompanied by a new realisation that God can act powerfully in and through us in spite of our weaknesses. Always there has been a sense of gratitude to God which wanted to express itself in prayer and praise – in Pentecostal experiences, in tongues. Aquinas called these moments *innovations*. Sullivan suggests we might translate that word as 'surprises of the Spirit'.

This second interpretation explains my own experience more satisfyingly than the first. When I was baptised in the Spirit in 1964, I did not relate it to my baptism in 1927 at all. Nor did it seem to have much to do with my confirmation in 1936, or my ordinations to the diaconate in 1952 and to the presbyterate the following year. It had more to do with a desire that, after years in which my ministry seemed to bear little fruit, God's power would be made more manifest through me. And I think my sentiments about it are not uncommon.

Pentecostal Baptisms

The second interpretation is, as we have seen, close to Pentecostal teaching on baptism in the Spirit. But we have to remember that, although they distinguish between water-baptism and Spirit-baptism as two events in a Christian's pilgrimage, they do not necessarily understand Spirit-baptism as a separate experience *chronologically*. The distinction is about our personal openness to the Spirit. Spirit-baptism usually follows conversion, but that is because of the way we respond to God. We need to repent before we can receive.

When Peter called on Cornelius and his household to have faith in Christ ('everyone who believes in him receives forgiveness of sins through his name'), the Spirit fell on his hearers (Acts 10:43–4). Whether the Gentiles had repented and come to faith before they were baptised in the Spirit is not the key issue. What is important is that coming to repentance and faith is logically separate from baptism in the Spirit. If conversion and Spirit-baptism occur more or less at the same moment, nevertheless conversion (or salvation, or regeneration) is distinct from and precedes Spirit-baptism.

This sequence is further implied in Paul's question to the Ephesians before he baptised them in water and laid hands on them: 'Did you receive the Holy Spirit when [or after] you believed?' (Acts 19:2) The apostle must have assumed that it was possible to repent and to believe in Christ without the accompanying reception of the Spirit.

Pentecostals insist, therefore, that Spirit-baptism is not about salvation. They do not imply that some Christians are only partly saved. They recognise that those of us who repent, affirm our faith in Christ, and are baptised in water are truly disciples of Jesus Christ. They also accept that our response to God's saving grace is a real impulse of the Spirit within us.

So to assert that Pentecostals have a two-stage process of Christian initiation is not strictly accurate. They simply maintain that Christians who only get as far as being converted have not been empowered fully by God for their Christian discipleship. Baptism in the Spirit is concerned with spiritual power, not salvation.

Only rarely is baptism in the Spirit associated with the baptismal liturgy. I once attended in a Baptist church the initiation of a woman who appeared to be baptised in the Spirit as she emerged from the water (she began speaking in tongues with great joy as the minister laid his hands on her head with a prayer for the gift of the Spirit). I have also met one or two Anglican bishops who say some candidates began speaking in tongues as they confirmed them. As a student of the liturgy, I could wish all Spirit-baptisms could be so arranged – preferably on Easter eve or Pentecost eve to fit in with the Church's calendar!

But the Spirit is not so liturgically minded. He comes to each individual when that person is ready or needful. The majority of Anglican Charismatics testify that they were baptised in the Spirit years after they had been baptised in water and confirmed. For some it is signalled by the gift of tongues; for others it is realised retrospectively as they come to recognise changes in themselves – or changes in them which are noticed by others.

The Doctrine Commission dislikes the phrase 'baptism in the Spirit'. In fact, they are quite rude about those who use it: 'Those who apply this term to this experience need to go to school with the Bible's own teaching on baptism in the Spirit.'[2] I felt embarrassed to be an Anglican when I read that. To imply that generations of Pentecostals do not know the Scriptures is discourteous, to say the least, in an official publication.

Whether interpreted as a receiving of more of what Christian initiation offers, or as a fresh sending of the Spirit into our lives, baptism in the Spirit has good scriptural foundations. It enshrines much that we still have to learn from Pentecostal spirituality, and I am not deterred by the Doctrine Commission's comment from using it.

And, in any case, the two theological interpretations of Spirit-baptism I have outlined are not so much opposites as complementary. In Christian initiation there is a sacramental sealing or a foretaste of the Spirit; but the fruitfulness of that anointing – as for all sacramental ministrations – will depend on our response to Christ, from the time of our initiation to the end of our earthly life.

In discussing Spirit-baptism we are struggling to explain the mystery of God's relationship with his people. We are talking about new encounters with the Lord Jesus Christ drawing us to the Father within the love of the Holy Trinity. However we explore that mystery theologically, what matters is that we keep in step with the Spirit.

As for the pastoral problem posed by a request for a second baptism, a solution can be found in the liturgical traditions of the Church. A renewal of baptismal vows with water has been practised in all ages – notably on Eater eve, when the whole congregation is sprinkled with water as a sign of their gratitude to God for their initiation into the Christian family, perhaps years previously.

I see no reason why this should not be adapted to meet the request I've just mentioned. I would explain to charismatically-renewed Anglicans that I cannot baptise them again according to the rites of the Church of England because that is not allowed for theological reasons. But since they have experienced a spiritual baptism, I would count it a privilege if I could join them in thanksgiving to God by performing a New Testament ceremony in water for them.

I would take them with the congregation to a baptistry where immersions can be performed (there should be one in each diocese). The service would include much praise and a sermon.

Then, after suitable prayers, I would dip the individual under the water, using words such as: 'N., in thanksgiving for your initiation into the Church, I immerse you in this water as a sign that, having died and risen with Christ, you have been anointed afresh by his Holy Spirit.'

I would not mention that the Greek word for 'I immerse' is the same as 'I baptise', *baptizmo*!

8

Confirmation

Confirmation has been a problem for the Church of England for most of this century. Almost every ten years or so a fresh debate has reared up among a cluster of questions: the right age for confirmation, the necessity of being confirmed before receiving Communion, the restriction of the rite to bishops, and so on.

Behind the debate is an uncertainty as to what confirmation really means. If it brings the gift of the Holy Spirit, in what way is that gift different from the gift of the Spirit in baptism? If it is not essential, why insist that everybody is confirmed before they can be regular Anglican communicants (which is distinct from the eucharistic hospitality offered to those who are communicants in good standing in other denominations)? If priests can confirm in the Roman and Orthodox Churches, why not Anglican priests?

We noted in the last chapter how in the West confirmation became detached from baptism and was eventually regarded as a separate sacrament. The anointing, or chrismation, which accompanied it in the medieval Church continues among Roman Catholics, but was abandoned by the English Reformers as an unscriptural and superfluous ceremony.

Retaining the episcopal laying on of hands, the Reformers utilised the occasion as a means of educating the youth in an outline of the Christian faith. The Prayer Book provided a catechism for this purpose. During the confirmation service, the candidates ratified publically the promises made for them at their baptism by their godparents. They then received the laying on of hands with a prayer that they might daily increase in the Holy Spirit. There are still Anglicans of an older generation who can recite the Catechism by heart and who tell stories about certain bishops who used to test the candidates' knowledge of it verbally during the service.

Catholic Anglicans stirred up the confirmation debate because they insisted it was one of the seven sacraments and that it sealed the baptised with the Holy Spirit. Besides appealing to patristic teaching and early liturgies, they cited Acts 8:17 (Peter and John in Samaria, a passage referred to in the Prayer Book confirmation service) and 19:6 (the twelve disciples of John the Baptist at Ephesus) as scriptural warrant. This became known as 'the Mason-Dix line' after two of its protagonists, A. J. Mason and Gregory Dix, who published books in support of it in 1891 and 1936 respectively.

Anglican Evangelicals and others were not persuaded. New Testament scholars favoured the view that the so-called 'confirmations' of the Samaritans and of the followers of John the Baptist were special occasions, when the apostles gave their approval by the laying on of hands to their followers' initiatives in baptising individuals belonging to communities outside Israel. They also cited the considerable evidence in the New Testament that the Holy Spirit is given in baptism. Other scholars – notably Geoffrey Lampe – demonstrated that the early patristic and liturgical evidence to which the Catholic Anglicans appealed did not substantiate their arguments as strongly as they claimed.

The pastoral consequence of this debate has been diversity of practice. In some Catholic Anglican parishes, children are confirmed at an early age so they can be admitted to Communion as soon as possible. In other parishes, particularly Evangelical ones, confirmation is used as an opportunity when young people, usually in their teens, make a public act of witness to their personal faith in Jesus Christ.

Growing ecumenical relationships have added further confusion to the debate. Evangelical Anglicans cannot see why those who have for years been committed Christians in a non-episcopal congregation should be expected to submit to confirmation if they have already been baptised as an adult. Surely these Christians received the Holy Spirit when they were baptised? And Catholic Anglicans know that in the Roman Catholic Church children are admitted to Communion before they are confirmed, and that it is permissible in certain circumstances for priests to confirm using oil blessed by the bishop.

Nowadays the Mason-Dix line has more or less been abandoned by Catholic Anglicans. There has arisen a broad ecumenical consensus that baptism in itself is the sacrament of initiation into the life of the Christian community, leading to the eucharist, the sacrament of abiding and growing in that life. Any attempt to argue that baptism is in itself incomplete is contrary to the New Testament. *Baptism, Eucharist and Ministry* is clear about this:

> The Holy Spirit is at work in the lives of people before, during and after their baptism. It is the same Spirit who revealed Jesus as the Son (Mark 1:10–11) and who empowered and united the disciples at Pentecost (Acts 2). God bestows upon all baptised persons the anointing and the promise of the Holy Spirit, marks them with a seal and implants in their hearts the first instalment of their inheritance as sons and daughters of God. The Holy Spirit nurtures the life of faith in their hearts until the final deliverance when they will enter into its full possession, to the praise of the glory of God (2 Corinthians 1:12–22; Ephesians 1:13–14). (pp. 2–3)

Responding to this document the Church of England admitted: 'Clearly the exact relation between baptism, chrismation, confirmation and first communion is not yet evident. There is confusion both in belief and practice in the Church of England...'

Liturgical Restoration

In the course of liturgical revision, the Anglican solution has been to restore the unity of baptism, confirmation and Communion in one service. In this believers' baptism becomes the 'norm' and infant baptism, followed by confirmation and Communion years later, is regarded as a variation of it.

The rites in the ASB are modelled on this plan, the unitary service of baptism, confirmation and first Communion being printed first and then separate services, including a service for the baptism of children, printed afterwards. A note in the ASB says that 'the bishop may anoint the candidates with oil which he has previously blessed for the purpose', though no prayer is provided for such a blessing (only the collect and reading for the eucharist at which the oils are blessed on Maundy Thursday). This is done in some Catholic Anglican churches.

The ASB rites have been welcomed in parishes where there is an increase in the number of unbaptised who are coming to faith in Jesus Christ and seeking admission to Church membership. The full service of baptism, confirmation and first Communion is a remarkably inspiring occasion.

Since the new rites came into general use, two other developments have complicated thinking about the role of confirmation. One is the small but increasing number of Church families who postpone the baptism of their children until the latter are old enough to make a personal response. This is due partly to these parents' doubts about the scriptural justification for infant baptism, and partly due to their hunch that in the kind of society their children will grow up in, it is better that they should receive this important sacrament as believers rather than as unconscious infants.

The other development is the growing practice of giving young children Communion at parish or family eucharists. The Church of England has gradually allowed this, individual bishops laying down conditions about some simple training beforehand. The result is that there are now teenagers, who come to church with their parents but who do not receive Communion because they have not been baptised and confirmed, while there are in the same congregation children – some as young as seven or eight – who have been baptised as infants and who receive Communion before they are confirmed. In such a diversity of practice the question is raised, what is the role of confirmation?

The pastoral assumptions behind the practice of confirmation have also been questioned in the Roman Church. There is increasing dissatisfaction with the custom of recruiting numbers of children and preparing them for confirmation in time for the bishop's pastoral visitation. It is felt that individuals need to be treated separately and confirmed when each is ready for it.

The Roman Church's *Rite for the Christian Initiation of Adults*, promulgated in 1972, has attracted much attention among Anglicans. The RCIA is a restoration of a fourth-century form of the catechumenate in which candidates are led through a series of steps to Christian initiation with the support of godparents, sponsors and the whole Christian community. It is seen as a process in which there is growing faith as well as personal instruction. Although intended for unbaptised adults, it is being adapted as a form of preparation for confirmation.

Following on from this, some Roman bishops have received permission from the Pope to allow parish priests to confirm their own candidates. The Roman Catholic Bishop of Salford introduced this policy in his diocese some years ago, accompanied by a carefully planned scheme of Christian education, or 'formation', for children and young people. His priests use oil which he blesses in his cathedral on Maundy Thursday. They can now exercise their personal judgement to administer confirmation when it is appropriate for each individual. Much of the preparation for confirmation is done by teachers and other trained laity in the parish, with the advantage of giving more attention to the individual needs of each candidate.

This flexibility highlights the importance of seeing the role of confirmation from the perspective of personal pilgrimages rather than admission to Communion. If confirmation is a sacrament in which individuals encounter Christ at a significant moment in their lives, then it should be related to the way in which the Holy Spirit is working in them and how they are responding to him. Otherwise to confirm children, teenagers or adults just because it is convenient for the bishop's diary is another example of over-sacramentalisation.

The type of society in which we live has made Christians realise all the more their need for the guidance and empowering of the Holy Spirit in every situation within which they find themselves. The forces of secularisation are probably more diverse and persistent than they have been at any other time in history. Certainly those who have close contact with young people in schools, colleges, places of employment and situations of unemployment, are aware of how much greater these pressures are on them than they were on similar age-groups thirty or so years ago. The breakdown of family and community structures adds to them.

This is one of the reasons why more people are seeking spiritual renewal, and why so many of the younger folk are discovering it in charismatic churches, networks and groups. They are thirsty for the waters of life in the deserts of the materialistic and scientific world, and God is graciously providing them with water from the Rock in a new Pentecostal outpouring.

What, then, is the role of confirmation in this scene today?

Confirmation and Ministry

If we see baptism as complete in itself, at whatever age it is administered, then that liberates confirmation from being tied to it. Confirmation instead becomes an occasion for marking a significant stage in the individual's Christian life – not initiation into that life, but another turning-point which is related to personal growth in spiritual maturity and service.

The lessons of the renewal are helpful here. The true sign of baptism in the Spirit is not the gift of tongues (though that can – and often does – have its own important role); it is in growing spiritual maturity and the willingness of the Christian to undertake significant acts of ministry in the Church and in the world. Once believers experience the power of the Spirit in their lives, they often become eager to take new initiatives or to tackle their existing ministries in a new way. They have moved over from a state of dependency on the Christian community to one of interdependency, with Jesus as the inspiration in their lives and relationships.

It is an appropriate time for them to be confirmed. They may not receive baptism in the Spirit when the bishop lays his hands on them (though this might still be the occasion for some new charism like tongues to be given), but they would receive recognition from the Church that they are now accepted as members with ministries.

This would dovetail with speculations about the role of confirmation which have been talked and written about for a long time. In 1944 a joint commission of the Convocations of Canterbury and York produced a report, *Confirmation Today*, which suggested that confirmation could be regarded as the ordination of the laity, and that it need not necessarily precede first Communion.

David Stancliffe, in *Liturgy for a New Century* (1991), argues that by detaching confirmation from baptism, confirmation would be more of a formal acceptance of one who has begun to accept responsibility for his or her part in the ministry and mission of the Church. It would be an authoritative commissioning for mission, renewed at each eucharist in the words: 'Send us out in the power of your Spirit . . .'.

Once it has been accepted that baptism followed by Communion is the basic rite of Christian initiation, this could be administered either to infants (with admission to Communion some years later) or to candidates who are old enough to answer for themselves. Hopefully the Church of England might then follow the example of some other Anglican provinces and provide a form of chrismation at baptism. This would strengthen the sacramental symbolism of baptism as not only a washing away of sin but also an anointing of those who are entering into the Spirit-filled life of God's own Anointed One.

Confirmation would remain as an episcopal rite alongside ordination as a ratification and commissioning of particular ministries. This is already being done in some dioceses where individuals are encouraged to undertake, after discernment and training, pastoral ministries of various kinds – teaching, counselling, praying for healing, deliverance ministries, and so on. Confirmation would become akin to what happens when members of another denomination are 'received into the Church of England'; they put their gifts at the disposal of the local parish.

It would reflect the current trend in ecumenical thinking to recognise baptism as complete initiation in itself, and confirmation as both an affirming of our baptism (in the case of infant baptism) and a public acceptance of the gifts we have to offer in the service of Christ's kingdom recognised by the Church's chief pastor with the laying on of hands.

And it would also give sacramental expression to the rise of the concept of an every-member-ministry, for which the charismatic renewal has been largely responsible. We shall discuss this in the next chapter.

Interestingly this pattern is assumed in the 1979 *Book of Common Prayer of the Episcopal Church of the USA*. In the baptism service in that book, the administration of the sacrament is followed by a chrismation in which prayer is offered that 'all who are sealed with the Chrism may share in the royal priesthood of Jesus Christ.' Admission to Communion follows, immediately in the case of a believer's baptism, later in the case of an infant's.

The service of confirmation is grouped, not with baptism, but with the bishop's offices. It has the character of reception and reaffirmation, and is clearly associated with the status of the candidate in the Church. The bishop's prayer for the candidates in confirmation refers to the sealing of the Spirit as an event in the past (at baptism) and there is no suggestion of a further 'dose' of the Spirit. Rather, the prayer is for renewal:

> ... by the sealing of your Holy Spirit,
> you have bound us in your service;
> renew in these the Covenant ...

Then comes the commission:

> Send them forth in the power of the Holy Spirit ...

> Strengthen, O Lord, your servant N with your Holy Spirit, empower him/her for your service; and sustain him/her ...

Confirmation in this form is therefore both a ratification of baptism and a public recognition of those messianic gifts which empower for active service – in other words, an acceptance of one who has been baptised in the Spirit to become part of the every-member-ministry which is the body of Christ. As David Stancliffe puts it:

> Confirmation has had a varied history, and different ages have slanted it in their own way. There now seems to be both a liturgical and ecumenical convergence on an understanding of confirmation which has to do with affirming our baptism, making public a commitment to the life of the Church and having gifts we offer in the service of the Kingdom recognized by the Church's principal minister. (p. 80)

Such a pattern would form a fitting framework for drawing together the sacramental sign of confirmation and the experience of baptism in the Spirit. Perhaps the day is not too far distant when the term 'laity' is abolished altogether, when it is recognised that through the anointing and empowering of the Spirit we all – present-day ordained and un-ordained – are ministers of Christ together. If the ordination of women succeeds in breaking through the 'clergy-line', maybe we are nearer to that united ministry than we dare to pray.

Every Member Ministries

The charismatic renewal appeared when the ecumenical movement had caused Christians to study, not only the reasons for
disunity, but also the nature of the unity to which Jesus Christ
is calling us. The biblical and liturgical movements were also
involved: the Scriptures as revelations of different models of
the Church; the liturgy as expressions of such models of the
Church at prayer. And, as we have seen, out of it came a new
understanding of the sacraments as encounters with Jesus Christ
through his Spirit within his Church.

Anglicans have always had a doctrine of the Church, of
course, but – like other Christians – it had been in the background of their teaching and preaching. They have tended to
see the Scriptures as the source of proof-texts for the model of
the Church which had evolved within the establishment. They
have had to defend their claim to being the Catholic Church in
this country against the counter-claims of the Roman Church.
And they have had to explain themselves as a Reformed
Church to the suspicious and anti-establishment Free Churches.

In 1920 the Lambeth Conference, in its appeal 'To All Christian People' for reunion, set out what the Anglican bishops
regarded as the four essentials on which the visible unity of the
Church must be based: the Bible 'as being the record of God's
revelation of himself to man, and as being the rule and ultimate
standard of faith'; the Creed; 'the divinely instituted sacraments
of baptism and Holy Communion'; and 'a ministry acknowl-
edged by every part of the Church as possessing not only the
inward call of the Spirit but also the commission of Christ and
the authority of the whole body.' Without calling into question the spiritual reality of other ordained ministries, the Conference put forward the claim that episcopacy was 'the best
instrument for maintaining the unity and the continuity of the
Church'.[1]

The document offered a very structural view of the Church. That was, perhaps, inevitable. Talks about unity always seem to revolve round questions such as those listed in the Lambeth Quadrilateral – the structures within which the Scriptures are taught, the sacraments are administered, the faith is professed, and the pastoral leadership is authorised. These topics – especially the ordained ministry – generated a long and far-reaching debate. The output of Anglican theological literature on ecclesiology was enormous. I will mention three of the many books representative of those themes which are relevant to our discussion.

Michael Ramsey's *The Gospel and the Catholic Church* (1936) is regarded as the most outstanding work on this subject up to that time. He aimed to show how the Church with its structures of sacraments and ordained ministry developed out of the Old and New Testaments, with one eye on the problem of relating the non-episcopal ministries of the Free Churches to the threefold ministry of the Anglican Church, and the other eye on the claims of papal authority in the Roman Church. He also discussed the liturgical movement which was just beginning to touch the Church of England, and he saw the celebration of the eucharist as the expression of the Church in a locality. He was not so concerned to examine the role of the laity in the Church.

After the Second World War, Anglican writers began to popularise the concept of the Church as the assembly of God's people. The biblical model of the Church as the body of Christ came to the fore. Representative of these writers was John Robinson with his book, *The Body: A Study in Pauline Theology* (1952) which discussed the reality and implications of our being 'in Christ'. With an ecumenical concern not unlike Ramsey's, he expounded the apostle's image of the Church as a body with many parts, a diversity within unity:

> It is worth noting how the fact of unity, as a basic datum, always stands for Paul in the main sentence; the multiplicity, on the other hand, is expressed by a subordinate phrase or clause with the sense of 'in spite of'. Thus: 'The members of the body, *being many*, are one body' (1 Cor. 12:12); Seeing that we, *who are many* . . . , are one body in Christ' (Rom. 12:5) . . . There must indeed be multiplicity if there is to be

a body – and it is observable how the great passages on the
Body are precisely in contexts which stress and demonstrate
the inevitable *diversity* of Christ's operations (1 Cor. 12: 4–13;
Rom. 12:3–8; Eph. 4:1–16). But the diversity is one that
derives from the pre-existing nature of the unity as organic:
it is not a diversity which has to discover or be made into a
unity. (p. 60)

One Body, Many Gifts

Robinson's book firmly established the 'body' image of the
Church in Anglican preaching and teaching. We are so used to
it now that it is difficult to imagine how novel it was in those
days. But his exposition about diversities within the unity of
the body could be applied, not only to different denominations,
but also to differences within a single congregation. Inevitably
this led to reflection on the role of the Holy Spirit in the
Church, for Paul's teaching about the body is, of course, closely
integrated with his teaching on the Spirit and his gifts.

So the charismatic nature of the Church came into Anglican
consciousness, though it was not initially called that. One sign
of this is in the third book, Alan Richardson's *An Introduction
to the Theology of the New Testament* (1958). This became the
basic textbook for a generation of Anglican theological
students. Here is what Richardson wrote as he followed up the
discussion in his Chapter 13 on 'The Apostolic and Priestly
Ministry':

> The Church is ministerial because Christ is Servant. The
> Church as Christ's body, the instrument of his purpose, con-
> tinues his apostolic and priestly ministry to the world. . . . It
> is not surprising therefore that the conception of Christian
> disciples as *ministers, servants*, should have received great
> emphasis in the early Church, or that baptism into the Church
> should have been regarded as an ordination to the ministry
> of Christ (1 Cor. 12:13 in its context). There are no 'lay'
> members of the Church who are without a ministry in it; the
> Church is a ministerial priesthood of the laity or people of
> God. We must not allow the development of a special order
> of *diakonia* to obscure the truth that the whole community

and every individual member of it were a ministry which participated in the one ministry of Christ. There are 'diversities of ministrations' in the Church, but all are performed to and through 'the same Lord' (1 Cor. 12:5). Every member of the Church receives his own 'manifestation of the Spirit' (1 Cor. 12:7) to enable him to perform his own God-given ministry: the Holy Spirit of God distributes his various *charismata* 'as he wills' (12:11). The whole passage 1 Cor. 12:4–30 makes it very clear that *diakonia* is not a function merely of certain 'orders' in the Church, but that every layman has his part in the total ministry of the body of Christ, which corporately through the empowering of the Spirit constitutes an organic ministry that renders service . . . to God. (pp. 304–5)

Anglican ecclesiology was moving beyond the institutional model of the Lambeth Quadrilateral to that of a living body with diversities of ministries among its membership. Free Church teachers could say that such a model had been held among their members long before Anglicans started talking about it. And the Prayer Book and the Articles reflect the biblical themes of body and fellowship. But such concepts were not at the forefront of Anglican consciousness until the teaching reflected in these books percolated through to parochial preaching.

While Anglican theologians were thus uncovering forgotten truths about the Church, 'God's frozen people', as one writer called them, were experiencing what it meant to be active as members of the body.

On the parochial front the sixties saw the arrival of 'Christian Stewardship'. Brought over from the USA by a fund-raising firm called the Wells Organisation, it was adopted in English churches as a scheme not only to raise money for parochial funds by regular giving, but also to encourage individuals to commit themselves under the headings of 'treasury, time and talents'. The spiritual basis of this was often lost in the business of reaching financial targets ('treasury'), but at least it sowed the idea that each number of the congregation has one or more 'talents' which the Lord could use in the Church, and that he or she should donate 'time' for the use of those talents for the common good. Parishes which used the scheme suddenly discovered a wealth of abilities among the laity which they had not realised before.

The Church of England also began to channel more resources into the further education of the laity. Specialists and teachers were appointed to promote what came to be known as 'laity development' within the dioceses. Catholic Anglicans borrowed the expression 'lay apostolate' from the Roman Church. Christian Institutes were established under a variety of names. Courses proliferated, using what were then new audio and visual aids. Pastoral counselling and the skills of leadership learned through experiences in group dynamics joined the topics of post-ordination and in-service training for the clergy and the laity. The ministry of spiritual direction began to be talked about and sought, especially in retreats.

In the meantime the changes in the Roman Church were having a knock-on effect, not only among Catholic Anglicans but also among Evangelicals as well. The Second Vatican Council's constitution *De Ecclesia* seemed to Anglicans a vindication of their own ecclesiology. Charismatics were delighted with the section on *charismata* expounded with great theological and ecumenical sensitivity by Hans Kung in *The Church* (1967). When David Watson was writing his widely read book, *I Believe in the Church* (1978), he told me that he had Kung's book at his side.

What Is Rigid Gently Bend

I have heard some Evangelical Anglicans say about their baptism in the Spirit that, among other things, it resulted in their 'conversion to the Church'. What they meant was that they became more aware of belonging to the body of Christ. Watson's book was the product of this awareness. They suddenly had a vision of the Church as more than a future community of born-again believers – what David Winter called 'the pot of gold at the foot of the Evangelical rainbow.' They saw it in more charismatic and sacramental terms.

The conference of Evangelical Anglicans at Keele in 1967 marked a turning-point, the majority of participants committing themselves to working within the Church of England and also within the wider ecumenical scene. By then the charismatic renewal was spreading among that constituency to give impetus to their intentions. Those who were at Keele have since remarked that there were many Charismatics among them, but they kept a low profile and were perhaps more influential as a consequence.

What baptism in the Spirit did for Catholic Anglicans was to present challenges of a different kind. Had they taught their flocks to be faithful church people rather than followers of Jesus Christ? Were they truly submitting to the Word of God in the Bible? What did their ordained ministry mean in relation to the spiritual gifts they saw the unordained laity exercising around them – often more effectively than they could themselves? Through the renewal, the Spirit began gently to bend the rigidity of some aspects of Catholic Anglicanism and, among other things, prepared them for the kind of reassessment of the sacraments which we are discussing.

So the charismatic renewal flowed over into a parochial scene in which many of the laity were already beginning to assume wider responsibilities than they had done before. What it did was to give us a fresh expectation that each Christian has a ministry or ministries to fulfil in the power of the Holy Spirit. There was a marked shift in outlook. It was realised that training and skills were not enough. Individual Christians had to be confident that being in Christ meant being open to the resources of his Spirit, for which baptism was a sacramental sign and baptism in the Spirit an experiential commissioning. Instead of talking about 'lay training' or 'stewardship', we began to hear about an 'every member ministry'.

The phrase came, I think, from the Pentecostal churches. For them it was a corollary to preaching the 'full Gospel'. I first heard it in renewal circles in the sixties. The novelty of it challenged me to study afresh what the New Testament taught about ministry in its widest sense.

For some Anglicans the phrase still sounds odd. To their ears 'ministry' (when not applied to some government department) refers to the vicar and his curate, or perhaps to the Free Church minister. They know what 'training for the ministry' means, and they are used to the categories 'laity' and 'ministry' from announcements at deanery and diocesan meetings.

As so often, it is largely a question of language. We are familiar with the designation 'servants of God'. Anglicans

are used to being called 'servants' in liturgical prayers, and to
thanking God for 'all thy servants departed this life in thy faith
and fear' (Confirmation and Communion services in the *Book
of Common Prayer*).

'Ministry' and 'service' are virtually interchangeable in the
New Testament. The passages on the gifts and ministries of
the Spirit came to have a reality far more profound than we
had realised: 1 Corinthians 12–14, where Paul teaches about
the charisms and their ordering; Romans 12:4–13; Ephesians
4:11–13; 1 Peter 4:10–11. The spiritual gifts range widely across
the life of the people of God: from prophecy to hospitality,
from uttering wisdom to interpreting tongues. The Corinthian
and Ephesian texts have been enormously influential in
reawakening this vision of the Church among all the main-line
denominations.

It has also, in a kind of reverse action, influenced the way
the Ephesian text is being understood. In the Revised Standard
Version of 1946 it was translated:

> [Christ's] gifts were that some should be apostles ... for the
> equipment of the saints, for the work of ministry, for building
> up the body of Christ ...

The meaning is that apostles, prophets, evangelists, pastors and
teachers have three things to do: to equip the saints; to do the
work of ministry; and to build up the body of Christ. Now
compare that with the New International Version of 1973:

> [Christ] gave some to be apostles ... to prepare God's people
> for works of service, so that the body of Christ may be built
> up ...

The three tasks have been reduced to two. The apostles, etc.,
are still to build up the body of Christ, as in 1946, but the work
of ministry is no longer theirs. Instead, they are *to equip the
saints for the work of ministry.*[2]

The Church of England has, of course, always recognised
spiritual gifts among its members. Innumerable Anglican laity
have manifested the power of the Spirit in every age (an aspect
of Church of England history which has yet to be researched).
In the seventeenth and eighteenth centuries the great missionary enterprises were founded, and a host of voluntary societies

provided many with the means of ministering in Christ's name to the poor, the sick, and the imprisoned.

By the end of the nineteenth century lay readers were taking services, and district visitors, Scripture teachers and Bible-women and other kinds of lay helpers were involved in parish work. Church conferences were summoned in many dioceses so that the laity could be consulted, preparing for the establishment of first the Church Assembly and then the General Synod in the following century. Every parish has its readers, church-wardens, secretaries of committees, vergers, cleaners, choir masters, musicians and choirs, servers, Sunday School teachers ... the list is endless.

But the charismatic renewal caused a paradigm shift in me and many other Anglican clergy. Meeting Christians of all denominations who had been baptised in the Spirit made me realise how much I had missed out both personally and in my pastoral ministry. To be an Anglican Christian meant much more than what I had expected. What the New Testament said about God's people was actually happening. They were living stones, a spiritual house, a holy priesthood, after all!

I felt like one of the crowd with Elijah on Mount Carmel. The wood for the sacrifice had been provided (in the kind of books I have just mentioned). The bull had been slaughtered (in the older Anglican concept of ministry). The water had been poured over the oblation (in the teaching about lay training – I will refrain from trying to identify the four hundred and fifty prophets of Baal!). Now all that was required was the fire from heaven. For me it came with baptism in the Spirit and the realisation that every member of the Church was potentially a minister.

As our congregations endeavour to open up opportunities for various ministries, considerable changes are taking place in traditional Anglican parish life. The priest is learning to share pastoral and spiritual responsibilities with lay people. Discernment becomes a key factor in leadership. 'Elders' are appointed in some parishes for laity who exercise leadership functions. 'Teams' are drawn together to accept responsibility for worship, evangelism, education, finance, buildings, and so on. Full-time and part-time posts are created in wealthier parishes, or subsidised in the poorer ones. New ministries are appearing as

Christians exercise gifts of healing, deliverance, and simple prophecy.

There's much to thank the Lord for in Anglican parochial life today. And there's as much for which we have to ask his wisdom and protection! Congregations caught up in these changes have to learn how to manifest the fruit of the Spirit as well as the gifts!

But that is not within the scope of our discussion. Rather, we have to ask, what do these developments in the recognition and enabling of a diversity of spiritual gifts mean for the administration of the sacraments in such parishes? And what is distinctive about the role of the ordained clergy in them?

Charisms for Ordination

To understand the relationship between the sacrament of ordination and the gifts of the Spirit, we have to see how ordination developed in the Church and how it came to be regarded as a sacrament which bestowed a permanent sacramental character on the ordained.

Out of the New Testament Church, with its variety of ministers and ministries, the threefold pattern of bishops, priests and deacons gradually took shape. There is documentary evidence to show that this pattern was established in many places where the Church spread round the Mediterranean world by the second century.

Initially the bishop seems to have been the chief pastor of a local congregation. But as the Church grew and new congregations were planted, he delegated responsibilities to his presbyters. They took over his ministries of presiding at the eucharist and baptising catechumens in the newer congregations, the bishop reserving for himself the final anointing and laying on of hands (the beginnings of confirmation). The deacons were the administrative officers of the bishop. In cities like Rome they became persons of considerable importance.

The bishop retained for himself the right to ordain deacons and presbyters in most places (in Alexandria at one time it seems as if the presbyters elected and ordained their bishop from among themselves). Only men were ordained to the episcopate and the presbyterate; women were ordained as deaconesses, though by the early Middle Ages that custom had disappeared.

This threefold ordained ministry adapted itself to all kinds of social and political situations. Certain bishops in key cities in the Roman empire – Alexandria, Antioch, Constantinople, Jerusalem and Rome – acquired a patriarchal status, the Bishop of Rome becoming the Patriarch, or Pope, of the West. In contrast, the diaconate dwindled until it became little more than a preliminary step towards the priesthood. The administrative officers of the Church who performed diaconal functions were ordained as presbyters. In England the archdeacon is nearest to what the deacon used to be in the Church of the first centuries – and he is nearly always a priest.

The words 'ordination' and 'orders' slowly acquired a sacramental meaning. They come from the Latin, *ordo*, which meant a particular class in the society of the Roman empire. The senators formed the higher order into which one was 'instituted' (Latin, *ordinari*). Everybody else belonged to the *plebs* ('the people'). When Constantine gave Christianity a privileged place within the empire, being 'instituted' or 'ordained' to the 'order' of office-bearer in the Church came to be seen as having social significance. Thus the distinction was created between the *ordo* and the *plebs* in the Church – or between the clergy and the laity. From that time the clergy began to wear a distinctive dress to mark their status.

Originally, then, ordination meant being appointed to an ecclesiastical office. It did not mean the laying on of hands with prayer. Appointments depended on the local congregation; they chose their pastors from among their number, or from those who were respected and well-known in the city or neighbourhood. But this should not be mistaken as an exercise of democracy in the first Christian communities. Rather, it was an exercise in corporate discernment of God's choice for a particular task in the congregation.[1]

The principle was distorted in later centuries as monarchs and others used their influence to make sure the persons they wanted were appointed to posts where they would be useful. Vestiges of this remain in the way the English monarch still has to approve the appointments to bishoprics and some other jobs in the Church of England.

Early Christian writings and the ancient ordination prayers reflect the belief that it was God who chose and ordained ministers. There was thus no dichotomy between what was done 'from above' and what was done 'from below'. Although the individual's own sense of vocation played some part, this might be overridden by the local congregation.

One of the most famous instances of this was the call and ordination of Ambrose to be Bishop of Milan in 374. When the previous bishop died, the laity in Milan demanded that Ambrose should succeed him. At the time Ambrose was only a catechumen. With some hesitation he accepted the call, but had to be baptised before he could be ordained. He proved to be one of the greatest bishops ever to pastor that particular see. The Milanese Christians had exercised their gift of discernment with prophetic insight. This contrasts sharply with the modern view that the most important element in an individual's ordination is that he or she should believe that they are being called by God.

When a bishop was ordained to be the chief pastor in a local church, the laying on of hands was performed by bishops from neighbouring churches. This served to affirm the acceptance of that local leadership by other local leaderships, and it helped to preserve the unity with the body of Christ. If you had assisted in the ordination of your neighbouring brother bishop, you felt in some measure responsible for him! It was only later, as the Church was organised on a territorial basis using some of the imperial boundaries, that dioceses became areas of episcopal responsibility.

The Roman Church in Italy today has about four times as many dioceses as the Church of England. In the smaller of these Italian dioceses, some of them embracing not more than a town with its surrounding countryside, we get a hint of how bishops in the early centuries ministered; they were more like rectors of large parishes than what we are familiar with in this country today. It was only later that parishes developed as areas of pastoral care for presbyters within a diocese.

Normally bishops, priests and deacons were appointed to Christian communities for life. Moving from one church to another was regarded as abnormal. But as the clergy emerged as a distinct group within the Church, and as they came to be regarded as having powers to preach the gospel and to administer the sacraments anywhere, they were appointed to different posts without further laying on of hands.

Ordination Rites

The first ordination rites included a period of prayer, either in silence or in the form of a litany, in which people offered to

God their petitions for those who had been chosen. These prayers culminated in a solemn oration recited by the presiding bishop. The oldest texts ask the heavenly Father to send the Holy Spirit to bestow the personal qualities necessary for the effective fulfilment of the office. They say little about what the newly ordained is to do.

But, as with the other sacraments, the understanding of ordination began to change. As the Church grew, it became more institutionalised. The hierarchy became more powerful. Bishops were seen as the focus of their diocese's sacramental ministry. The recital of the prayer by the bishop with the laying on of hands came to be regarded as the sacramental sign which 'made' the candidates ministers, and their election by the congregation as merely a preliminary. The prayers themselves were affected by this change: besides asking that the priests and bishops might grow in holiness, they also ask for the gift of the Spirit with power to fulfil the office itself.

With an increasing body of canon law to support him, the role of the bishop in the administration of the sacraments was vital. He and his brother bishops were accepted as the successors of the apostles, and the laying on of hands symbolised the continuity of the Church's ordained ministry in an apostolic succession (see Appendix 2). The congregation were now little more than onlookers in the whole process of choosing and ordaining their pastoral leaders.

So it was that the word 'ordination' came to mean, not the appointment to an office in the Church, but the rites themselves. The laying on of hands with prayer was regarded as bestowing a sacramental character on the candidates with a permanent spiritual seal, like the baptismal seal. What had begun as the discernment of a spiritual gift was changed into the administration of a sacrament.

However, the ancient understanding of ordination has not been completely lost. In the ASB ordination service, the congregation still has an opportunity to say that they discern the necessary spiritual gifts in the candidates for ordination. The bishop presents the candidates to the people, saying:

Those whose duty it is to inquire about these persons and examine them have found them to be of godly life and sound learning, and believe them to be duly called to serve God in this ministry. Is it therefore your will that they should be ordained?

People: It is.

Bishop: Will you uphold them in their ministry?

People: We will.

Although now embedded in the liturgy as little more than a formality (I suppose one day someone did in the past or might in the future lodge an objection at that point in the service, but I've never heard of that happening and I can't imagine it ever would!) it is a relic of the congregation's role in ordination. In some Anglican provinces the congregation is invited to reply 'in a suitable manner', which might be clapping, cheering and shouting, 'He's okay!'

The questions put to the candidates and the prayers offered for them refer to the tasks which the new deacons, priests and bishops are expected to fulfil in the Church; but there is still a strong emphasis on the need for them to grow in holiness in their personal lives. And they are invited to affirm their sense of vocation:

> Question: Do you believe, as far as you know your own heart, that God has called you to the office and work of a deacon (priest, bishop) in his Church?
>
> Answer: I believe that God has called me.

Ordination and Canon Law

Another relic of the corporate responsibility which the congregation once had for its clergy is in the provision of a 'title' (Latin *titulus ecclesiae*). Today this simply means that a post is available to provide a salary for the newly ordained, normally in a parish (the conditions are set out in canon C5 of the Church of England). Bishops are reluctant to ordain anybody without that provision, for obvious reasons. But its original purpose was to demonstrate that a congregation accepted the one God was calling to serve them – including his material wellbeing.

This obligation was enshrined in canon 6 of the Council of Chalcedon (451): 'No one may be "ordained" priest or deacon ... unless a local community is clearly assigned to him, whether in the city or in the country.' It comes as a shock to those who insist on the necessity of episcopal ordination to realise that, according to a later provision in this canon, ordination without such an appointment was rendered null and void, even if the candidate had received an episcopal laying on of hands.

Although priest's orders are regarded as indelible, he may not exercise a ministry without being licensed by a bishop of the diocese concerned. When a priest 'resigns his orders', he does not cease to be a priest. Canon C1 states:

> No person who has been admitted to the order of bishop, priest, or deacon can ever be divested of the character of his order, but a minister may either by legal process voluntarily relinquish the exercise of his orders and use himself as a layman, or may by legal and canonical process be deprived of the exercise of his order or deposed finally therefrom.

In other words, he no longer has the right to fulfil that ministry. This is also the practice (though without doctrinal reasons) in the Methodist, United Reformed and Presbyterian Churches.

This indelible, sacramental character of ordination was one of the factors which served to 'sacerdotalise' the ordained ministry. The title of 'priest', first given to the bishop (sometimes 'high priest') and then transferred to the presbyter, collected Old Testament analogies to itself and widened the gulf between the ordained and the laity.

> Although no early Christian document uses the title 'priest' directly to designate any Christian minister, from the beginning of the third century such language starts to emerge. This marks the inception of a major change in the relationship between the people and their ordained ministers: the latter will eventually cease to be seen as the presiders within a priestly people, and will become instead a priesthood acting on behalf of others.[2]

'Sacerdotalisation' increased in the Middle Ages with the distinction which was made between the power of the ordained ministry, particularly the power to celebrate the eucharist, and the jurisdiction, the legal rights to exercise that power (whether for a bishop in his diocese or a priest within his parish). Ordination was understood as a ritual process whereby an individual was given divine power to perform sacramental rites. Much canon law was drafted on this basis.

This distinction remains within the Church of England. That is why a priest does not normally administer the sacraments outside his parish, without the permission of the other parish priest or the bishop. And it is why the administration of the sacraments is restricted to the ordained ministry (except baptisms in an emergency).

My experience of the charismatic renewal gradually caused me to rethink what I believed about myself as 'a priest according to the order of the Church of England' (to quote the ordinal). I became uncomfortable with what seemed to be a cult of the priesthood in some Catholic Anglican circles.

I recognise that this concept of priesthood has been a precious vision in the lives of countless numbers of clergy. It has inspired heroic ministries on behalf of others and martyrdom for the kingdom. But that is true of many non-ordained Christians who have ministered in the power of the Spirit as well. If a priest is a 'walking sacrament' (a phrase often used in Catholic Anglican circles), then I feel that is also an appropriate description of every baptised and Spirit-filled Christian.

The Prayer Book retained the word priest both in the ordination service and in the administration of baptism and Holy Communion. The phrase 'parish priest' is interwoven with English culture and language. The distinctiveness of the clergy has been reinforced by the position they have held in society as representatives of the establishment. The ASB, however, uses 'presbyter' as an alternative.

I look forward to the day when all titles ('reverend', 'canon', 'venerable', 'very reverend', 'right reverend', and so on) disappear. It will do something to rescue the clergy of the Church of England from the social framework into which many of them are forced by the circumstances with which they are surrounded. I never use my title unless I have to for purposes of courtesy. Equalisation of stipends for all full-time posts would also help.

Abolishing the Laity?

In England bishops and priests have fulfilled a variety of roles. Besides being chief pastors in dioceses, bishops have been officers of state, foreign ambassadors of the monarch, feudal grandees and military commanders (the Bishop of Durham defended the northern border against the Scots up to the eighteenth century). Today they can be heads of organisations (the South American Missionary Society has a bishop as its chairman) as well as assistant diocesan bishops and pastors in parishes.

Besides working in parishes, priests have been – and still are – chaplains in schools, colleges and hospitals, principals of educational institutions, teachers and lecturers, missionaries and evangelists, on the staff of organisations and area secretaries, writers, journalists, broadcasters and welfare officers, and other things as well.

But the distinction between the ordained and the unordained remains firmly embedded in Anglicanism. The unordained may have the spiritual gifts for various ministries, but they are not admitted to orders. The ordained, on the other hand, remain priests for the rest of their lives so that, even if they cease to function as pastors, they can – if they have the opportunity – take up that ministry again.

What emerges from our brief review, then, is that ordination has collected to itself various elements: the discernment and acceptance of a charismatic gift of pastoral leadership in an individual by the Christian community; prayer by that community for further gifting by the Spirit so that the individual may be sanctified to make him worthy of that leadership and for all it entails; and the laying on of hands by the chief pastor accepting the gift and authorising its exercise on behalf of the wider Church. Once ordained, the deacon, priest or bishop was never re-ordained because it was believed that he had received at his ordination a spiritual seal endowing him with a permanent sacramental character.

The balance between discerning the charism and bestowing the authority has frequently been distorted. But since in an ordination we are responding to the call of God, discerning the gifts of the Spirit, and acting in union with Jesus Christ as members of his body, we are encountering a mystery in which distinctions are impossible to make. Yet there is scope for much further development in the concept and use of the sacrament of ordination.

Indeed, some would argue that any Church member who had the spiritual gifts could be invited to exercise the leadership of the ordained ministry when it was appropriate to do so. Alan Kreider, the Mennonite theologian, has contributed a persuasive essay entitled 'Abolishing the Laity' in *Anyone for Ordination?* (1993, ed. Paul Beasley-Murray). In it he draws a picture of local churches in which all gifts are discerned and used, and in which ordination to leadership is 'relative' and not 'absolute':

> There is no necessary reason to assume that a person who has been an effective 'overseer' or 'counsellor' or 'community involvement instigator' will continue to be equally effective in these roles forever, or if he or she should move to a different congregation. The Holy Spirit, who gives gifts, can revoke gifts. Congregations, and especially designated leaders, should be sensitive to this – alert to members who are ministering in ways that appear self-aggrandizing. Furthermore, congregations differ. It is therefore not helpful to view 'ministers' as transferable functional components. When they move to a new congregation, they should be subject to processes of gift discernment along with other members. If their gifts are affirmed, they may be re-commissioned in their new congregation. (pp. 102–3)

Such a suggestion will, I imagine, send shivers down the spines of my clerical contemporaries! We have assumed that a call to the ordained ministry is lifelong – protected by the doctrine of the sacramental priestly character. But if Alan's vision is beyond ours at the moment, the notion of flexibility which he advances is not quite so far beyond our reach in the Church of England. There are the first tentative signs of it as we seek to follow the Spirit today.

11

Local Ministries

A few years ago I attended two ordinations. The first was on a Saturday morning in an Anglican cathedral, when a friend was ordained to the diaconate. The congregation filled the nave, and the ordination was celebrated with a ritual precision and musical taste for which the cathedral is famous. I met my friend with his family afterwards to congratulate him, and he went off to attend his first service that evening in the parish to which he had been appointed as a curate.

The second ordination was the following Sunday afternoon in the New Testament Church of God at Old Trafford. When I arrived some young people were rehearsing hymns and choruses on a variety of instruments in the brightly painted building. I had been told that the service would begin about 3 o'clock, but I was familiar enough with that congregation not to be surprised when the hour came and went before the pews started filling up. Eventually a group of ministers from other NTCG churches ascended the steps to the rostrum and the service began.

After much praising, some prayer, a Bible reading and a sermon, Charles and his wife stood before the District Overseer, who was surrounded by a group of pastors from other parts of England. Charles made a simple testimony of his faith and call from God. Prayer was offered spontaneously for the sending of the Holy Spirit. The District Overseer and the pastors crowded round to lay hands on Charles, and he was given a new Bible. Then Charles' wife was also prayed for and blessed. There was more praising. When the service ended, I joined the congregation for tea in the church hall.

The contrast between the two services could not have been greater. The serene and ordered atmosphere of the cathedral was as different as anything could be from the exuberance and joy of the NTCG celebration. In the cathedral I saw only two or three black faces, in Old Trafford there were only a few whites. The cathedral felt 'institution'; the Old Trafford church felt 'family'. Within those few days I had shared in liturgies of contrasting cultures and ecclesiastical traditions. Yet at the heart of both was the same recognition of spiritual gifts and the same enactment of sacramental rituals: the praise of God through Jesus Christ and the laying on of hands with prayer for the Holy Spirit to equip my friends for their ministries.

Let me say that I appreciated both services. I enjoy – if that's the right word – Anglican cathedral worship (though I wouldn't want to attend to the exclusion of anywhere else). I also enjoy the Pentecostal celebrations of the black churches (though ditto). But that's not the reason I've described them. What intrigued me most was the different routes by which those two men had come to their ordinations.

Charles' ministry had been discerned and tested during the several years he had cared for a congregation in north Manchester. He had been sent there by the Old Trafford church to draw together a few members in that neighbourhood to see if he had the gifts to build it up into a congregation. That he had done. His ministry had been discerned and tested. Now it was recognised and ratified by the laying on of hands. Members of his congregation were there that Sunday afternoon to rejoice with him and his wife. The new Anglican curate went to his parish as a comparative stranger after his ordination. He had met some of the congregation briefly when he visited his future vicar one weekend, but that was all the contact they had had with him.

The black pastor had been 'on the job' for years; the Anglican curate had done nothing like it before in his life. If one of the early Fathers had been involved in the selection and training of those two men, I've no doubt that it was Charles' route to ordination which he would have recognised as nearest to his own. To him, the Anglican route would have seemed rather odd and unscriptural.

What has changed, as we saw in the last chapter, is that the Church of England depends heavily on the sense of personal call in the candidate for ordination and on the needs of the Church nationally. A typical scenario is that when Anglicans feel they have a vocation, they go to talk to their vicar about it. The vicar may – or, more likely, may not – discuss this with others in the parish. (In the parish where I live, a small group meets each candidate informally and reports to the clergy.) If the vicar thinks the vocation might be genuine, he contacts his diocesan bishop. The bishop may meet the candidates, or he may pass the matter on to his director of ordinands. The candidates are sent to one of the selection conferences arranged by the Church of England's Advisory Board of Ministry. From then on, if they are accepted, they are more or less certain to be trained and ordained unless they change their mind. It is not unlike embarking on any professional career.

Under this system, theological colleges are subjected to a subtle pressure to keep their students and do all they can to see they get ordained, for the colleges are in a competitive market, which depends on their attracting and retaining enough students to finance their establishment. I'm not saying that the principals and their staffs deliberately do this. They occasionally advise a student that in their opinion he may have mistaken his vocation and suggest he leaves. But that doesn't happen very often. Their basic inclination is to help the student finish the course and to find a job. Getting students through to what they are training for is regarded as the mark of success in a theological college as in any other further or higher educational institution.

This process of selection and training has evolved to provide the Church of England with a steady flow of spiritually and theologically equipped men and women for the many posts which have to be filled each year. And it has been reasonably successful in fulfilling the task it was set up to do. But now, through the 'thawing' of the laity and the spread of the renewal, the Holy Spirit is raising up men and women with gifts of pastoral leadership and discernment within congregations, and we are struggling to enable them to fulfil their ministries, though often hampered by the structures of the Church of England, where sacramental ministries are trapped within an outdated, geographical parochial system.

Around us, other denominations are more flexible. The New Churches, for example, are developing forms of training which are designed to equip those who are already involved in pastoral leadership within their congregations. Their modules put evangelism and apologetics much higher in the syllabus than Anglican theological colleges do.

In *Springboard for Faith* (1993) Michael Green, who for many years was a theological college lecturer and a principal, is critical of the present system. He thinks that attempts to regard theological colleges as adjuncts to universities prevent them from preparing students for the kind of pastoral leadership needed in the Church of England today. He contrasts that with his own recent experience in Canada:

> I have made it a rule for my students at Regent College, Vancouver, that nobody should graduate from the course without having been out with me in evangelising, and standing up to the objections of those who did not believe the Christian faith. This immediately had three effects. It raised the profile of the subject. It equipped people on the job. And it brought about a climate of intercessory prayer, an awareness of the spiritual battle, and carefully-honed preparation into the college, as people prepared to go out on mission. The sad thing is that few colleges today teach apologetics or evangelism, and even fewer have their instructors go out with their students into the chill winds of the agnostic world to learn by doing. (pp. 170–1)

Non-stipendary Ministries

Since the sixties the Church of England has gingerly embarked on a number of schemes to open up its pastoral leadership so that the sacrament of ordination can be offered more freely where spiritual gifts are discerned among its people.

The rise of the worker-priest movement in the Roman Church in France during and after the Second World War roused much interest in the Church of England, and in 1960 Mervyn Stockwood, Bishop of Southwark, set up the Southwark Ordination Course to train men and women for ordination on a part-time basis. Other dioceses copied SOC and now there are fifteen similar institutes for training in the country. All of them have students who are taking courses for lay as well as ordained ministries – an admirable policy for breaking down the clergy-line.

Years later the bishops issued regulations about what was first called the Auxiliary Pastoral Ministry and then in 1987 the

Non-Stipendary Ministry (NSM). Under this scheme, men and women are trained and ordained to exercise their ministry while continuing in their secular occupations.

The major weakness of this scheme is due to the muddled expectations that the Church of England has about the role of an ordained man or woman in secular life. Anglicans still persist in regarding a priest as a sort of super Christian. They cling to the medieval view that because a man or a woman has been endowed with the sacramental character of ordination they are more effective evangelists and counsellors than the laity. Ordain them, put them in an office or some other work situation, and they will 'be the Church' there, serving their fellow employees in the name of Jesus Christ.

The other expectation – that the NSM will be a valuable assistant to his vicar in the local parish – is, of course, theologically justified. A priest exercises his ministry of pastoral leadership in the Church wherever that leadership is accepted in Christ's name. Elsewhere – what we usually call 'in the world' – he is only significant as a leader of a religious community or sect within our secular society. His ordination, as a sacramental character, means nothing, for secular society has no recognition of Christian sacraments. Any other view is over-sacramentalisation.

I'm not saying that a NSM cannot act as an evangelist or as a counsellor in her work situation. Of course she can! And her experiences in that work situation will equip her to discern the ways in which God is active in the world, and to relate what she discerns to the gospel. But that will be because she has the gifts of an evangelist or a counsellor, not because she has been ordained. The only way in which her ordained status becomes relevant in a work situation is if she becomes the leader of the Christians there and presides over sacramental rites with them (such as lunch-hour eucharists or hearing confessions). Some industrial missioners fulfil this role, as do ordained teachers and lecturers in schools and colleges. Otherwise the ordained person cannot do any more than any other Christian at work. And, if she doesn't have the requisite gifts, she may be less effective. What we need in work situations and in society generally to lead people to Jesus Christ is not more ordained parsons but more Spirit-filled Christians.

Locally Ordained Ministry

A more hopeful sign is the development of the Locally Ordained Ministry (LOM). In 1987 the bishops of the Church of England issued *Guidelines for Local Non-stipendary Ministry* to help dioceses devise patterns appropriate to their own situations. These guidelines are aimed at a more charismatic model of ordained ministry, based on the relationship between the ordained person and the congregation of which he is a member. They state that the distinctive marks of this form of ministry are to be as follows:

1. The call of God to this ministry comes to the candidate, in the first place, through the local congregation of which he is a member . . . Ordination is the Church's validation of this call, to which the individual has responded.
2. A locally ordained minister exercises this ministry as part of a team of people, ordained and lay, working together in the same parish or locality.
3. This team may include lay people, with whom the locally ordained minister has trained.
4. The training of a locally ordained minister pays particular attention to . . . the local situation.
5. The ministry is local, in that it is confined by Licence.

The scheme is being launched in an increasing number of dioceses. It has varied results. But it provides a splendid opportunity for parishes to discern and affirm a form of pastoral leadership within groups, communities and congregations which is closer to the model behind the second of the ordination services I have described at the beginning of this chapter. It reflects the older understanding of ordination. It could be the means whereby the Church of England extends its ordained ministry beyond the boundaries to which that ministry has been confined for centuries. It could enable men and women whom the Holy Spirit has raised up as elders within congregations to be affirmed sacramentally by the Church. The United Reformed Church has such an eldership alongside its full-time elders and, as far as I can judge from my knowledge of them, it seems to work admirably as long as congregations accept their different gifts and roles.

It is important that the locally ordained minister has a strong congregational base: a vicar who can oversee her training and who can cope with a collaborative style of ministry; church members who are spiritually mature enough to be able to help her develop her gifts and rescue her from her mistakes; and, in the end, a decision-making process which, listening to God, can give her opportunities to take new initiatives or, if necessary, advise her that her ministry lies in another direction.

Attempts to encourage the LOM within tiny congregations in urban or rural areas without support from neighbouring parishes in the deanery have not so far been too encouraging. A situation can arise where the locally ordained minister is regarded as the supplementary priest with the vicar and the one-man-band becomes a two-person-band. That is fine if they have gifts which enable them to minister together to see the congregation grow spiritually and perhaps numerically; but not otherwise. On the other hand, locally ordained ministers could provide appropriate pastoral leadership in church plants or other ministerial or evangelistic groups.

Deacons

I do not see much future in the recent attempts to revive the permanent diaconate. It has been used as a probationary step towards the priesthood for too long. Canon C3 indirectly assumes this: 'A deacon shall not be ordained to the priesthood for at least one year, unless the bishop shall find good cause for the contrary, so that trial may be made of his behaviour in the office of deacon before he be admitted to the order of priesthood.'

In the Church of England the diaconate has been used in recent years, not so much to make the local church more of a serving ('diaconal') community, but to bring women over the clergy-line in preparation for their eventual ordination to the presbyterate. Women deacons have demonstrated that they can be pastoral leaders in parishes, but it was frustrating for them to have to import a male priest to preside at the eucharist. I doubt whether many of these ordained women will want to remain in the diaconate now that the presbyterate is open to them – demonstrating, surely, that there is little need for that order in the Church today.

The revival of the diaconate in the Roman Church is flawed for similar reasons. In spite of the scholarly appeals to the early Church's precedents, and the glowing accounts of what deacons are able to do in parishes where there are no priests, the impression I get is that in reality the diaconate is being used in the Roman Church as the Anglicans have used it – to bring those who cannot be ordained at the moment (in this case married men) over the clergy-line. If the Roman Church ordains married men, then the order of deacons will cease to have any significance in their congregations, too (unless they use it to bring women over the clergy-line as the Anglicans have done – a not impossible scenario). It will slide into the background as nothing more than a step towards the presbyterate – as it has been for centuries.

An every-member-ministry requires far more flexible and varied forms of ordained pastoral leadership than has been possible within the parochial system. It has to be much more of the people, for the people and by the people, rather than locked into the institutional mechanisms which are designed for self-preservation but little else.

But things are changing. The authors of the report, *The Priesthood of the Ordained Ministry* (1986) by the Church of England's Board for Mission and Unity, urged that we should seek to develop 'one corporate ministry and mission in which all the baptised share' (p. 18). An earlier report, written by John Tiller for the Advisory Council for the Church's Ministry, expanded the concept in the following statement: 'Baptism does . . . include an authorisation to minister as a Christian, and ministry is in fact more than a role: it is a way of being the Church, the means of expressing that care for others which is the true "agape" at the heart of the Christian life' (p. 66).

This is a very New Testament view of a congregation. And it cannot be fulfilled without a more charismatic administration of the sacrament of ordination. Gifts of leadership and enabling need to be recognised and affirmed through ordination as the Spirit leads the Church of England into new ways of evangelising and creating Christian communities in the country. It will change radically the relationships between bishops and their clergy, and between clergy and their congregations. Less institutional, more family.

In Acts 6, when the Greek widows were overlooked in the

daily ministry, the twelve did not wait for their relatives or for someone moved by pity to do something for them. What they did was to regard this as an opportunity for a creative expansion of their own ministry and they instituted an extension of it. They did this in consultation with their fellow believers. They left the process of selection to God through the congregation and continued with their own ministries, simply affirming those who had been chosen with prayer and the laying on of hands.

As a result, seven men were enabled by the Holy Spirit to begin by caring for the needs of the Greek widows but were then led to other ministries – Stephen to a preaching ministry so powerful that he became the first Christian martyr, Philip to an evangelistic ministry which helped to spread the gospel far beyond the bounds of Judaea.

If the Church of England can keep in step with the Spirit, the results could be in the same apostolic proportions. And she would be keeping in step with the thinking about ministry which is to be found in all the denominations – a triumph for a truly biblical theology of the Church, a theology which Anglicans have always claimed was theirs.

12

Eucharistic Praise

The effect of charismatic renewal on a congregation is usually noticed first in its style of worship. Congregations are said to be 'into renewal' or 'going charismatic' when a music group supplements or displaces the organ and choir with songs, hymns and choruses. The result is enlivening or lamentable according to one's point of view. Traditionalists in the world of church music scornfully call such congregations 'clappy-happy' parishes.

Like most general impressions, the false is well mixed with the truth in this picture. Choruses, rhythmic clapping, and up-lifted hands can be genuine manifestations that a congregation – or, at least, many members of it – are finding a new freedom in the Holy Spirit. But these manifestations may also be nothing more than attempts by the vicar or the singing group to brighten up the worship. Not that there's anything wrong in bright-ening up Church of England services. Many of them need it! But singing choruses enthusiastically is not necessarily indicative of anything much else.

The first attempt to integrate free-wheeling styles of worship with the Anglican liturgy usually means replacing hymns with modern songs and choruses. At a eucharist they are inserted at fixed points: at the beginning, between the readings (where a modern version of a psalm can be appropriate), during the offertory and the administration of Communion, and at the end. Quieter pieces can form an acceptable devotional accompani-ment as communicants go to and from the altar rail. Praise choruses replace the Gloria, which is after all, just a popular canticle from the early days which has got stuck as a semi-permanent element in the rite, and songs like Graham Kend-rick's 'We believe' are sometimes used instead of the Nicene Creed.

Many who are experiencing personal renewal in the Spirit

welcome these innovations. The 'worship group' as it is called (a misnomer if ever there was one: surely the congregation is the worship group?) has encouraged a flexibility in the liturgy which the ASB intended it to have but failed to achieve. Suddenly we have realised the value of the Liturgical Commission's care in limiting the mandatory parts of the ASB to a minimum, and in publishing further worship material and suggestions for creative liturgy in *Patterns for Worship* and *The Promise of His Glory*.

Evangelical Anglicans have found the meaning of the eucharist enriched in ways which Catholic Anglicans of previous generations had discovered through reviving traditional ceremonies; and both have drawn nearer to one another in their understanding of the sacrament of the Lord's Supper. We shall discuss this theological convergence in the next chapter. For Charismatics there is a growing perception that the eucharist is an act of praise and thanksgiving in which hearts as well as minds are lifted up to the Lord because of what they experience of the Spirit in their daily lives. Lifting hands in the air expresses what we feel as well as what we believe.

This posture, which is assumed by the president at the eucharist when he stands at the altar, is an ancient attitude of prayer. It is mentioned in the Scriptures and portrayed among the murals in the catacombs of ancient Rome, showing that this is how Christians in the early centuries prayed. It is known as the *orans* ('praying') position. Kneeling and prostration were for prayers of penitence and petition. Hands were lifted up for adoration and praise.

There may have been a connection between the *orans* and the laying on of hands. Many have discovered this when they stand to minister to someone. They raise their hands at the beginning of the prayer and then instinctively lower them onto the head or shoulders of the one they are praying for. This may have been the way in which what began as a devotional gesture, to accompany the prayers said over the newly-baptised and the newly-ordained, came to be perceived as a sacramental sign.

The charismatic renewal has helped many to rediscover the centrality of praise and thanksgiving in private prayer and corporate worship. Suddenly we respond with a new delight to these expressions of devotion in the Bible. The books of the Old Testament are full of praise. Israel believed that the whole of life was to be an affirmation of God's presence and will, and that his glory is the goal of creation.

> My mouth will speak in praise of the Lord.
> Let every creature praise his holy name
> for ever and ever. (Psalm 145:21)

God was also praised for his faithfulness and loving-kindness to the people whom he had chosen. The psalms recalled the mercies of God to Israel in the past, and looked for a continuation of that mercy and protection in the future. Because of what God had done for Israel, other nations would come to join in their praises as well.

Christian Praise

In the New Testament the praises of God continue, using psalms and forms of thanksgiving from the Old Testament, but now culminating in gratitude to the Father for the manifestation of his love in sending Jesus Christ as Saviour. Some of the apostolic letters open with ascriptions of praise, which may have their origin and inspiration in the prayers offered by the early Christian communities in worship:

> Praise be to the God and Father of our Lord Jesus Christ, who has blessed us in the heavenly realms with every spiritual blessing in Christ.
>
> (Ephesians 1:3)
>
> Praise be to the God and Father of our Lord Jesus Christ!
>
> (1 Peter 1:3)

The worship of heaven which John saw in his vision was one of angels and elders praising God with the *Trisagion* hymn ('Holy, holy, holy . . .') from Isaiah 6:3 (and Revelation 4:8, etc.). This vision may have been drawn from what he experienced in worship during his lifetime.

Many of these Old and New Testament texts are the inspiration for the thousands of new songs which have been published in the wake of the renewal. The desire to praise God is flooding over in the composition of them. Not all are written by Charismatics. But a high proportion are – many by young people, who have been baptised in the Spirit and who want to express a new joy in the Lord and their hopes and desires as disciples of Christ. Indeed, in most guitar groups it is likely that one or two members will have a go at writing their own pieces and trying them out at a family service.

The shelf-life of the majority of these songs is brief. If I say that poetically and musically most of them are not worth remembering, I'm not being deliberately unkind. A song written by an individual for a particular congregation may be the most appropriate vehicle for enabling those people to praise God on that occasion. Pierre Gelineau has said:

> The context in which a song is sung . . . often has more influence on the people's reactions than the song itself . . . The aesthetics of a song is not only to do with the quality of the text and the music, but with the whole ethos of the celebration of which this song is a part. A very simple tune can be dismissed as worthless if taken in isolation, but can make a marvellous contribution to the spirit and beauty of the celebration.[1]

Nevertheless, such pieces rarely stand much chance in competition with many of the fine hymns and choruses which are to be found among the collections now available.

The New Testament theme of thanksgiving to God for his redemption in Jesus Christ and the outpouring of his Holy Spirit is the dominant note in these compositions. Christians see themselves as recipients of a renewing of God's grace in the deserts of modern society and in the spiritual dryness of the modern Church. The prophecy of Isaiah rings with particular relevance: 'See, I am doing a new thing . . . I provide water in the desert . . . to give drink to my people, my chosen, the people I formed for myself that they may proclaim my praise' (Isaiah 43:19-21).

The use of these new songs as an integral part of the liturgy was a natural progression. Years ago, soon after I first heard the chorus, 'Holy, holy', I saw it as a fresh setting of the Sanctus. One day I was presiding at a eucharist in church and saying the introductory passage ('Therefore with angels and archangels and with all the company of heaven, we proclaim your great and glorious name, for ever praising you and saying . . .') when the words and music came into my head. On the spur of the moment I began singing it, and I was moved at the joyful and enthusiastic way the congregation joined in.

Of course, numerous modern settings of the eucharist have been available since Geoffrey Beaumont produced his *Folk Mass* a generation ago. But the experience I have just described was memorable because it was the first time I had encountered a spontaneous burst of praise breaking into the recital of the eucharistic prayer. Until then that prayer had been for me a solemn formulary, which the celebrant recited or intoned without any variations except those provided in the proper prefaces for feast days and seasons like Lent.

In the last ten years or so a new way of using these songs has spread through charismatic churches. Several songs and choruses – sometimes up to ten or a dozen – are sung one after the other in a kind of necklace of praise, which moves through various thoughts and moods led by the music group. This form of extended praise was introduced into England by John Wimber and the Vineyard Christian Fellowship, who have been immensely influential in charismatic circles since the death of David Watson.

For those who have not been initiated into this kind of worship, the effect can be off-putting. Everybody around you is standing, some with arms outstretched in a very un-Anglican fashion, while from the front of the congregation a group of musicians drift from one song to the next, usually with no announcements. If you don't feel like joining in, or if you don't know the songs (when I first encountered the Vineyard's worship in the early eighties, the songs were completely new to me) you feel very much left out of things.

However, once I learned some of them, and discovered that the purpose of the laid-back presentation of these songs, one after another, was to encourage the congregation to focus their minds and imaginations on praising God, I began to join in. I found that, if I set aside my Catholic Anglican ideas of what an act of worship should be like, and my fear of what those around might be thinking of me, I could enter into these sessions of praise in a deeply meaningful way. In terms of Christian spirituality, I have heard the experience described as a corporate act of contemplation.

Eucharistic Prayer with Songs

This kind of praise can be applied to the expressions of thanks-giving within the eucharistic prayers – not only those in the ASB but also those provided in *Patterns for Worship*. In the latter book there are a further four alternative eucharistic prayers, numbered A to D, which are designed to give more participation for the congregation than those in the ASB. An explanation of their origins together with guidance on how to use them is contained in the introduction to the book.

To illustrate how Vineyard-type praise and the text of the eucharistic prayers can be woven together, I ought to explain the purpose and structure of these prayers. They normally include:

1. An opening dialogue, with the versicle and response, 'Lift up your hearts' – 'We lift them to the Lord.'

2. An introduction to praise with words such as, 'It is indeed right, it is our duty and our joy, at all times and in all places to give you thanks and praise . . .'

3. An extended act of thanksgiving which can include refer-ences to the many things for which we can praise God. These variations are called 'proper prefaces' ('proper' = the right or appropriate reference for the occasion; 'preface' = the beginning of the prayer). The earliest eucharistic prayer known to us, that of Hippolytus dated about 215 AD, was a framework which the bishop used freely, adapting the text as he wished, and the proper prefaces are thought to be formalised versions of what was once the bishop's free prayer. Presidents of Anglican eucharists are now learning to offer their own prefaces spontaneously and, in small groups, to invite the worshippers to add their informal thanksgivings at this point, too. The act of praise culminates in the Sanctus.

4. The narrative of the institution. This is almost invariably set within the prayer in the Orthodox-Catholic liturgies, but there are some eucharistic rites in which it is read as a text to announce the biblical authority for the celebration before or after the prayer.

5. The memorial prayer, summing up the mystery of salvation in the death and resurrection of Jesus. It may include more

detailed aspects of the work of salvation up to and including the Second Coming.

6. One or more prayers asking the Father to send the Holy Spirit both on the bread and the wine that they may be sacramental signs of the body and blood of Jesus Christ, and on the communicants that they may grow in holiness and unity with one another.

7. The concluding doxology. This is the high point of the prayer. It is a proclamation as well as a profession of faith. It also makes a climax of what we might call the sanctifying movement of the prayer, since in this doxology the divine name is pronounced in its fullest and most explicit form.

Not all these elements are included in every prayer, and sometimes the order is changed. In Alternative Eucharistic Prayer C, for example, the Sanctus is transferred to the end of the prayer.

The most satisfactory way of blending songs and choruses with the eucharistic prayer is to choose with sensitivity those which echo or respond to the thoughts and joys of each element in it, then to sing those pieces whilst the president pauses and joins in himself.

Some of the songs take their inspiration from the same texts of Scripture which inspire the prayers. Isaiah 6:3 and Revelation 4:8 are obvious examples. References to creation, the incarnation, the cross, the resurrection, the ascension, the gift of the Holy Spirit and other saving events can be matched with songs on these themes inserted at appropriate sections in the prayer.

I have found that, after rehearsals with the music group and explanations to the congregation, it is possible to lead the worshippers in a eucharistic prayer which is interwoven with singing. The effect is to surround the recital of the prayer (or its intonation – though that is more difficult if the music groups have to adapt to key changes) with an aurora of song which lifts hearts as well as minds to God in an extraordinarily moving way. It brings into the central prayer of the eucharistic celebration the spirit of contemplative praise which I have just described. (I have given a couple of examples of how this looks on paper in Appendix 3.)

Teaching and Worship

Once parishes have begun experimenting with this kind of celebration, they will soon be led into other ways of incorporating contemporary Christian praise into liturgical worship. I'm not into Christian rock, so I can't make suggestions in that direction!

However, this kind of presentation of the eucharist is not for everybody. I'm sure it will never replace the quiet said service, the sung parish communion, the cathedral eucharist, or those more exotic occasions, like the mass I attended in the Austrian capital with music provided by the Vienna State Opera chorus and orchestra. But it is one way in which charismatic praise, which might include singing in the Spirit, can be harnessed to the sacramental worship of the eucharist, bringing experience and liturgy together in an enriching manner.

And it is important that what is experienced charismatically by individual members and groups in the Church of England should be associated with what is instituted for worship in the past and reformed in the present. This is one of the ways in which the energies generated by spiritual renewal are directed into the upbuilding of the Church rather than the fragmentation of its fellowship.

What I am suggesting is a coming together of sacramental doctrine and charismatic gifts in an experience of worship – an example of how theology can be put to work to glorify God. The same principle can be applied to other spiritual gifts and sacramental signs – movement and dance, the touch of the ashes on Ash Wednesday and the wood of the cross on Good Friday. The possibilities for revitalising traditional liturgical gestures and symbols are boundless, drawing on what the Synod report called the inchoate sacramentalism of Pentecostalism. The release of the Spirit brings to life the experience of worship contained formally within the liturgical rite.

Tom Smail made this point in *The Giving Gift*:

The eucharist, like the Church in which it is celebrated, is *instituted* by Jesus. Without that historical givenness it loses its context and its meaning. It is *constituted*, however, by the Holy Spirit. Without him it lacks, so to speak, its *con* factor, the togetherness of head and body, and remains simply a

commanded ordinance. The Spirit takes what Christ instituted and involves us in it, so that he is present with us to
give and to receive, and we are present in him to receive and
to give. (p. 195)

Harnessing the charismatic to the liturgical can often lead to
a deeper appreciation of traditions of worship. Just as some
people – especially among the young – will begin with contemporary art forms (music, art, architecture) but then discover
more of what is worthwhile in the past, so it can be with church
services. Individuals who found a freedom in spontaneous
prayer begin to see old formularies with new eyes. Many charismatic prayer groups have been introduced to Taizé chants via
quiet chorus versions of the psalms, and some have from there
gone on to plainsong.

There has also arisen a new appreciation of the literary
beauty of the Prayer Book Holy Communion service, which
has nothing to do with preserving our ecclesiastical heritage,
but everything to do with discerning how the Holy Spirit speaks
through what has been handed down to us from the past.
Schooled in ways of heartfelt worship, they learn how to use
what is of the Holy Spirit in the old as well as in the contemporary as they offer themselves, their souls and bodies, in love to
God the Father through Jesus Christ.

13

Spirit and Eucharist

I have already suggested that the process of liturgical revision in the Church of England ran parallel with the spread of the charismatic renewal, and that I believe both movements are signs that the Holy Spirit is equipping God's people for their worship and mission in the future.

In producing *Lent, Holy Week and Easter* (1984), *Patterns for Worship* (1989) and *The Promise of His Glory* (1990), the task of the Liturgical Commission is subtly changing. Instead of being a committee which draws up services for authorisation by the bishops and the General Synod, it is also becoming one which provides liturgical resources for groups, parishes and large assemblies generally in the Church of England. These books, properly used, are helping Anglicans to discover the renewing grace of the ministries of Word, prayer and sacrament, as we saw in the last chapter.

One fruit of this grafting of liturgical revision into charismatic renewal is a new understanding of the role of the Spirit in the celebration of the sacraments. I have already discussed this in relation to baptism, confirmation and ordination. I now want to explore it a little further in relation to the sacrament of the Lord's Supper. I shall use as a contemporary source of the Church of England's doctrine on this topic the new eucharistic prayers in the ASB and in *Patterns for Worship*.

In doing this we are treading on delicate ground. The doctrine of the eucharist has been a centre of controversy among Anglicans since the outbreak of the ritual troubles at the end of the nineteenth century and the events leading up to and beyond the attempted revision of the Prayer Book in 1927–8. It was revived briefly in the Synod debates authorising the ASB. This controversy has circled round the questions of what we mean by the eucharist as a sacrifice (an attempt to introduce the phrase 'we offer' into the prayer was rejected) and the bread and the wine as signs of Christ's presence.

The sharpness of this controversy has been blunted by the convergence of views about the sacraments as a result of the ecumenical movement. As I have already said, this convergence has had an internal effect on the domestic differences in doctrine which we have within the Church of England. Evangelical and Catholic Anglicans have been willing to try and learn from one another.

Other factors were that Evangelicals themselves, through membership of the Liturgical Commission and of the General Synod, were closely involved in the discussions surrounding the new rites and, to a lesser extent, realised that within their own tradition there was a greater appreciation of the richness of eucharistic theology than they had realised. Similarly, Catholic Anglicans have been influenced by the reassessment of sacramental teaching and practice in the Roman Church up to and following on from the Second Vatican Council.

With this background, I now want to show how Evangelical and Catholic Anglicans are finding their experience of the Spirit is drawing them closer together in eucharistic doctrine than they have been before. To adapt the old adage, *lex orandi* is having its effect on *lex credendi*.

The Liturgical Commission drafted the texts of the new eucharistic formularies on the fundamental principle that when we pray according to the teaching of the New Testament, we address ourselves to the Father in union with Jesus Christ by the power of the Spirit. Prayers addressed to Jesus tend to be of a more informal, personal nature. In liturgy it has been the ancient and universal practice to address the Father within the Holy Trinity.

One result of the charismatic renewal, as we have seen, is to give Christians a greater sense of the reality of the Holy Spirit and of the Holy Trinity. Many Charismatics will say that, after they had been baptised in the Spirit, they became aware in a new way of the Fatherhood of God and of the sacrifice of his Son for their sins. In fact, a charismatic experience which does not lead to a deep devotion to God as Creator and Jesus as Saviour and Lord is gravely immature. Leaders in the renewal constantly remind us of the social implications of following the

Spirit and of the presence of Christ crucified in the sufferings of humanity as well as glorified in his Church.

The Trinitarian basis of the eucharistic prayers, therefore, acquires a vital relevance. They express the truths that we look to the Father as both the origin and the fulfilment of what we are celebrating, that our offering is only possible because of our union with the incarnate Son, and that the Spirit supplies the strength of love which makes our offering possible and makes it effective in our lives. This pattern is clear, e.g.:

Father, we give you thanks and praise... Your beloved Son... was sent by you... send the Holy Spirit... (ASB, p. 136)

By presenting us with a variety of these prayers, the Commission is able to give recognition to different aspects of the eucharist – its cosmic range, its redemptive purpose, and its eschatological scope, and to set the celebration within the whole action of God in creation, reconciliation and consummation.

The parts of the eucharistic prayer which express what we believe we are doing when we break bread together are the prefaces, the invocation of the Spirit on the worshippers (known as the *epiclesis*) and the memorial prayer ('Remembering his offering of himself...', known as the *anamnesis*). These are places where we see signs of the Evangelical-Catholic convergence.

Thanksgiving

The references to God as Creator are based on the biblical revelation that the physical universe belongs to God, and is therefore good, although spoilt by sin, tragedy and death. The Spirit renews our awareness of the sacredness of creation with all that implies. In the eucharistic celebration creation itself, represented not only by ourselves as worshippers but also by the bread and the wine, is seen as worshipping its Creator in a kind of everyday festival:

The fruit of the earth itself praises you:
Wheat and grape, this bread and wine we have,
are part of the riches of your earth. (*Patterns*, p. 239)

Evangelical and Catholic Anglicans alike have welcomed the opportunities to worship God creatively in the eucharist. Evangelicals are being liberated from their suspicion of ritual and introduced to all kinds of accompaniments to the eucharist – some traditional, some novel. In this they find they have much in common with Catholics who are seeking to update older ceremonies and symbols. One small indication of this is the widespread use of the cassock-alb and the stole (which some Evangelicals still prefer to call a 'coloured scarf'!).

Thanking God for what he has created involves us with our fellow human beings of all nations and races who, like us, are made in the image of God. It also makes us conscious of our stewardship of the earth, and of the vastness of the universe; and we are alerted to the need to preserve what God has made and protect it from pollution and exploitation.

All things are of your making,
all times and seasons obey your laws,
but you chose to create us in your own image,
setting us over the whole world in all its wonder.
You made us stewards of your creation,
to praise you day by day for the marvels of
    your wisdom and power:
so earth unites with heaven
to sing the new song of creation. (*Patterns*, p. 192)

To worship the God of righteousness is to commit ourselves to being signs of that kingdom in our relationships with one another in his family, in our love for our fellow human beings, and in our willingness to struggle for justice and equality:

Lord God of justice and mercy,
    you care for the world and for each of us;
    we glorify your name . . .
Help us to work together for your kingdom
and for the day when your justice and mercy
    will be seen everywhere.

Such a commitment is a genuine sign of renewal in the Spirit, for it is a consequence of responding to the love of God for his world; and we can join with and learn from other Christians who pursue the Lord's mission in justice, peace and the integrity of creation.

All the eucharistic prayers centre on the cross, as did the prayer of consecration in the Prayer Book; but they also spell out the blessings of his sacrifice through his resurrection, ascension and the gift of the Spirit – though the reference to the latter is usually in the *epiclesis*.

Through him you have freed us from the slavery of sin,
giving him to be born as man and to die upon the cross;
you raised him from the dead
and exalted him to your right hand on high.
                    (ASB p. 133, etc.)

For our sins he was lifted up
that he might draw the whole world to himself . . .
Unite in his cross
all who share the food and drink
of his unending life. (*Patterns*, p. 245)

So the eucharist is a 'perpetual memory of his precious death' and also a celebration of all the saving events of the gospel. It is also a foretaste of the heavenly banquet, shared with him until he comes again. The Spirit points us beyond this world to the second coming of Christ and the consummation of his kingdom:

Until the kingdom of God comes
we keep the feast which he began.

The Prefaces

The prefaces echo the major themes of biblical pneumatology – the sending of the Spirit on Jesus at his baptism, the sending of the Spirit on the Church at Pentecost, and the sending of the Church in the power of the Spirit for mission and service in the world. There are two prefaces which have a distinctly charismatic flavour.

How wonderful are the works of the Spirit,
revealed in so many gifts!
Yet how marvellous is the unity
the Spirit creates from their diversity,
as he dwells in the hearts of your children,

filling the Church with his presence
and guiding it with his wisdom!

You have given all peoples your Holy Spirit
who works marvels by innumerable gifts,
distributes an abundant variety of graces,
gives us to announce the Word in various tongues,
gathers us together in unity,
remains in all believers,
and fills and governs the entire Church. (*Promise*, p. 233)

Sometimes, when I have presided at eucharists where Charismatics have been in the congregation, I have sensed them
beginning to respond as I have spoken such words as these.
They have begun singing in the Spirit or crying out 'Alleluia!'
as if such texts are ignition sparks for bursts of spontaneous
praise. In *Patterns* (pp. 168–189) there are numerous biblical
responses which could be used at such moments. One of the
longer acclamations might have come from the Vineyard Christian Fellowship with its 'signs and wonders' form of evangelism:

You shake us and fill us with your Spirit,
you stretch out your hand to heal,
to do signs and wonders through the name of Jesus.

Scripture has always been a major source of liturgical prayer
– doctrinal themes, salvation history, poetic and prophetic literature, symbols and images. In *Patterns* the Liturgical Commission
goes further than any other revision I know by offering biblical
passages for use verbatim as prefaces for eucharistic prayers:
Isaiah 53, John 1, Romans 8, Colossians 1 and others. It
resembles the way Scripture is often used at prayer meetings.

Invocations of the Spirit

It is the wording of the invocation of the Holy Spirit (*epiclesis*)
over the bread and the wine and the phrasing of the memorial
prayers (*anamnesis*) which are most sensitive in the debate
between Evangelical and Catholic Anglicans, because these sen-
tences express what we think the eucharist is and what we
believe the Lord is doing when we celebrate it. And it is in
these two places in the prayers that the role of the Spirit

does much to remove causes for misunderstanding. For the invocations of the Spirit underline the truth that we are utterly dependent on the grace of God in our worship.

They show that in the eucharist we have access only through Christ to the Father by the Spirit, and that the communion of the body and blood of Christ is possible only because Jesus is made present by the Spirit in the sacramental signs. We encounter Jesus Christ, not because we use certain words or formularies, but because the Spirit acts to reveal Christ through the sacramental actions.

> Grant that by the power of your Holy Spirit
> these gifts of bread and wine
> may be to us his saving body and blood. (ASB, p. 131)

The *epiclesis* over the bread and the wine has a special significance. Through the renewal Evangelical and Catholic Anglican Charismatics are familiar with invocations of the Spirit on persons, actions and things in other situations – in prayer groups, in the ministry of healing, in projects for service and evangelism, and so on. These experiences give them a fresh perspective on the presence of Christ in the sacrament.

For Evangelicals discerning the body and blood of the Lord need not be overshadowed by anxieties about the doctrine of transubstantiation. The *epiclesis* firmly establishes the mode of Christ's presence as a manifestation of the Spirit – a spiritual gift through an inanimate object. For Catholics the *epiclesis* means that the bread and the wine become the outward and visible signs of Christ's body and blood, not because the priest recites a liturgical formula over the elements (though church order in these matters is important), but because God responds to our prayer and, by the mysterious action of his Spirit, makes these elements inward and invisible vehicles of his presence.

This shift of perspective has another consequence. Like other young Catholic Anglicans, I was taught to regard the reserved sacrament as a means of encouraging devotion to our Lord, both in private prayer and in services of benediction. I certainly used to find it an inspiration to kneel near an aumbry or a tabernacle in church; it gave me a focus of attention on the Lord, no matter how unprayerful I felt.

In the years after baptism in the Spirit, however, I had more faith in the Spirit's visitation wherever I was. I still believe that

Christ is present in the sacrament, but I also believe he is present by his Spirit in many other ways, too – in the Scriptures and among his people. Of course, I cannot speak for others. The service of benediction has been in the programme of some charismatic conferences I've attended. Accompanied by singing in the Spirit, it is a beautiful act of worship. But I have the impression that devotions before the reserved sacrament are not now so central in the prayer life of Catholic Anglicans as they used to be.

Presence and Memorial

Belief in Christ's presence in the bread and wine is linked with the doctrine of the eucharistic sacrifice; and the nature of that sacrifice is expressed in the *anamnesis*, where we describe what we are 'remembering' when we 'do this in remembrance of me.' The memorial of Christ is celebrated with a recognition that it is in the Holy Spirit that Christ unites us with his offering. As a consequence, although we offer 'ourselves, our souls and bodies' to God the Father, our offering adds nothing to the efficacy of Christ's offering on the cross, since our action is only possible in him because his sacrifice has been completed once and for all.

In *Patterns* the memorials reflect this interpretation. They assume that what we are doing is not just an act of remembering the sacrifice on the cross but a 're-calling' of that sacrifice so that its blessing becomes a reality by the power of the Spirit among us.

> Pour out your Holy Spirit
> as we bring before you these gifts
> and remember his sacrifice
> made once for all on the cross. (p. 250)

Instead of the controversial 'we offer', the Liturgical Commission has opted for the alternative, 'we plead'.

> Father, we plead with confidence
> his sacrifice made once for all,
> we remember his dying and rising in glory,
> and we rejoice that he prays for us at your right hand.
> (p. 244)

Again, as in our understanding of the mode of the sacramental presence, it is the experience of the Spirit which throws new light on the sacrificial character of the memorial. Evangelical and Catholic Charismatics are familiar with spiritual gifts as a 're-calling' of the ministry of Christ in the Church today, for the same Spirit who anointed Jesus in the Jordan equips his people in every age. In the same way, then, through the *anamnesis* we ask him that we might share sacramentally in his Passover. The time-leap is vividly realised in one eucharistic prayer, which has a preface taken from the Jewish Passover blessings.

> Blessed are you, Lord God of the universe,
> you bring forth bread from the earth . . .
> Blessed are you, Lord God of the universe,
> you create the fruit of the vine . . . (p. 239)

These could have been the actual words used by our Lord in the upper room when he took the bread and the wine and 'gave thanks'.

In the new rites, then, we have admirable vehicles for offering our praise and thanksgiving to God within the eucharist, putting behind us the controversies of the past and looking for the renewal of the Church's life and mission from her worship today and in the future. If Anglican Charismatics are tempted to copy the worship they encounter in independent Pentecostal-type fellowships, they should also realise what is available in their own traditional and contemporary rites. These new churches may have something to teach us about free-wheeling praise of God. But their worship is often impoverished liturgically because they have little discernment of the Spirit's gifts for worship in the past and in the wider Church. That is why we should make full use of what the Commission is providing for us.[1]

14

Sacraments and Charisms on the Way

So far we have discussed the effect of the charismatic renewal on our understanding of the sacraments of baptism and the eucharist, and on confirmation and ordination. To complete the picture we should now briefly bring into our review the ministry of reconciliation, anointing of the sick, and marriage. These sacraments mark our encounters with Jesus Christ at particular moments in our spiritual pilgrimage, so they are best seen within that context.

What many Christians realise after they have been baptised in the Spirit is that events in daily life gradually acquire a greater significance. Things no longer happen accidentally or coincidentally. We are more aware of the Spirit's guidance and opportunity.

This expectancy is derived from Pentecostal spirituality, where the individual's responses to the Holy Spirit are marked by mountain-top experiences. The Everest among these is Spirit-baptism; but life is punctuated by other experiences, too – miraculous encounters, deliverances from evil, gifts of healing, inexplicable events which disclose the hand of God, prophetic utterances, and so on. These experiences are, of course, highly personal, but they leave a growing conviction of the reality of God's presence. Life is lived in a gospel dimension, the Lord working with us and confirming the work with signs following.

At first sight this seems to contrast with traditional Anglican spirituality, which sees our pilgrimage as one of slow but steady growth with its ups and downs. Evangelical Anglicans remember their conversion. Catholic Anglicans remember their confirmation and first Communion. But the expectation of both is that their spiritual growth is promoted through the discipline of daily prayer and Bible reading, regular attendance at church, and occasional visits to conferences, retreats, rallies and other faith-building events. Many find it helpful to have a rule of life.

Within this supporting framework, Anglicans make the dozens of decisions each day which, if made in obedience to Jesus, enable them to grow in grace and slowly become more and more conformed to his image.

Another feature of Pentecostal spirituality is noteworthy. In communicating the gospel the spiritual histories of individuals, groups, communities and congregations play a key role. That is how the early Pentecostals did their theology. The exposition of biblical texts in the light of personal experiences of the Spirit's power is characteristic of their sermons and books. Everyone has a story to tell, showing that God is the God of the here and now. God speaks, he acts, he equips his people as he did in the New Testament Church. The title of the magazine of the Episcopal Renewal Ministries in the USA is *Acts 29:* that title proclaims the Charismatics' belief that our stories are a continuation of the narrative of the Church in Acts.

When this Pentecostal spirituality is expressed in prayer, we are struck by its immediacy and relevance. God is addressed as One among us. Nothing is too minor to be unworthy of his attention. Jesus is Lord over the most minute matters of daily life. Someone happens to ring up with an item of news – that was the Lord's timing. Someone else drops by with a bag of tomatoes – that was the Lord's gift. Every day there are miracles in miniature.

Such an attitude, adopted from the Pentecostals, can expose Charismatics to ridicule. We've all heard about the parking place which was amazingly available in answer to prayer! Trivialisation there may be, but didn't the Lord say that the hairs of our head are numbered?

Encountering such an expectation can make Anglican spirituality seem tame indeed. Yet when we look at Pentecostal and Anglican traditions more closely, we find in fact that there are strong parallels. Strip away the cultural packaging and there is revealed a biblical foundation which is common to both.

Take, for example, the apparent contrast between Pentecostal mountain-top experiences and Anglican inner spiritual growth. The Pentecostal preacher will often find it necessary to remind his congregations that Christian discipleship has its periods of desert dryness and spiritual warfare as well as moments of divine presence and power. There are times when the Lord seems absent; his disciples have to hang on to the memory of what he has already done and the hope of what he has promised. The praise-centred worship with its triumphalist prayers is designed to support the weak as well as encourage the strong.

Penitence, fasting and spiritual warfare; acts of self-examination and confession; the hymns which echo the psalmist's doubts, fears, reproach and despair; Scripture readings which touch every aspect of life: Pentecostal spirituality is as well aware of these themes as Anglicans are when they keep the season of Lent.

And Anglicans, too, can have their mountain-top experiences – moments when Jesus was very close in an act of worship, such as the Easter eucharist on a bright spring morning; the pilgrimage to Iona or Lindisfarne, Wells or Walsingham; making one's confession after a long lapse; sacred moments during a quiet day or a retreat. But in our tradition we are afraid of saying anything about them in case we are regarded as pious cranks. The difference is not so much that Anglicans don't have mountain-top experiences than that we're not taught to expect them, recognise them, and share them.

So the Anglican encounter with Pentecostal spirituality has been enriching. The Pentecostal stress on living life today in New Testament terms has brought Anglicans close to the Christianity of the apostolic authors. Since our Church claims to look back to the early Church as its model, this has been an eye-opener to what that claim means.

Reconciliation

And when we fail, both Pentecostals and Anglicans know the need to repent. Here the Anglican ministry of reconciliation, as confession to a priest is called nowadays, could teach Pentecostals how the sinner may be assured of God's forgiveness. Although only a minority of Anglicans make their confessions as a regular discipline, many more – and not only Catholics – resort to it in times of crisis.

The absolution formula pronounced by the priest, 'I absolve you in the name of the Father and of the Son and of the Holy Spirit', has been the subject of theological debate. It was laid down as the proper form for the sacrament in the Middle Ages, when the theology surrounding the practice was complicated by ideas about indulgences and penitential exercises. It was rejected by the leaders of the Reformation as an unacceptable expression of priestly power. In view of this it is surprising that it remained in the Prayer Book in the service for the visitation of the sick.

More recently theologians have stressed that, when a penitent is absolved, he or she is not only forgiven by God but also restored to fellowship with the Christian community. Like the other sacraments, there has been a recognition of the role of the Holy Spirit both in the gift of repentance and in the assurance of reconciliation to God and to the community.

The Liturgical Commission has put forward a version of the absolution formula which expresses this ecclesial – Church-related – nature of reconciliation and modifies the 'I absolve' phrase:

> God, the Father of all mercies,
> through his Son Jesus Christ
> forgives all who truly repent and believe in him:
> by the ministry of reconciliation
> which Christ has committed to his Church,
> and in the power of the Holy Spirit,
> I declare that you are absolved from your sins,
> in the name of the Father, and of the Son,
> and of the Holy Spirit.

Lent, Holy Week, Easter where this prayer is to be found (p. 56), includes suggestions for services of penitence which can be a wholesome variation to those which focus solely on praise. A congregation which is open to the Spirit will be convicted of sin as well as strengthened in faith.

But I think I'm expressing the views of many penitents when I say that, although the ministry of reconciliation leaves me with a sense of thankfulness for the forgiveness that Christ won for me on the cross, it does not always assure me of the Spirit's armour to fight against temptations in the future. Even the prayer just quoted only speaks of the power of the Spirit in which the absolution is announced.

Nowadays when I hear an individual's confession, I lay hands on his head after the absolution and ask God to fill him afresh with his Holy Spirit through the death and resurrection of Jesus. In Chapter 3 I described one such occasion. The house which has been swept clean from sin needs to be filled with the goodness of God. The laying on of hands for spiritual renewal is appropriate. Liturgical scholars tell us that absolution was given in this way before the invention of confessional boxes which screen the penitent from the priest and make the gesture impossible.

For a long time the ministry of reconciliation has been linked with spiritual direction, another name for the exercise of the charism of discernment. Both the ministry of inner healing and the deliverance ministry are also related to forgiveness, and the renewal is helping us to learn more about these today, in spite of mistakes and excesses which sometimes accompany them. In the deliverance ministry especially, there is an increase in the use of such sacramental signs as the crucifix, holy water and blessed oil.

On the day the General Synod finally ratified the legislation for the ordination of women, Ruth Gledhill, the churches' correspondent of *The Times*, described how she made her confession to a Synod member, Sue Hope, who was then still in deacon's orders. The journalist wrote: 'Laying her right hand on my head, she prayed for healing. Even though technically not absolved, I still felt in some way healed, and cried all the way back to the office' (24 February 1994).

Healing and Wholeness

This illustrates how the ministry of reconciliation is intimately linked with that of healing, where the influence of Charismatics in the last three decades has been considerable. There is a renewed faith that by his Spirit Jesus Christ brings gifts of healing in answer to prayer to the sick, even when they have not been cured through normal medical and nursing care.

Of course, no responsible teacher in the healing ministry fails to emphasise that anyone who is ill should always follow the advice of the doctor. Also, we should not underrate or overlook the gifts of healing which God offers through simple, human, commonsense things, like prolonged rest, care offered by others, sorting out relationships, being relieved of stress, and so on.

Having said that, however, Charismatics still believe that there are occasions when the Lord, for his own mysterious purposes, stretches out and heals some directly in answer to prayer where medicine has failed; and that for many others the healing process is speeded up through such a ministry. But this means they also have to be sensitive in ministry when healings do not take place. The words 'miracle' and 'miraculous' are used too freely by some, creating incredulity rather than faith.

The renewal has brought a fresh impetus to anointing with the laying on of hands, which Catholic Anglicans revived at the end of the nineteenth century. As we have seen, Brother Bill was one of the first Anglicans in this country to recognise the role of Pentecostal gifts in healing. It is yet another example of how sacramental sign and spiritual gift belong together.

Today many parishes regularly have services of prayer for healing in one form or another. In a number of churches pairs of lay 'ministers' make themselves available to pray with people during or after the Sunday services; in others they have been trained to take Communion to sick and housebound members after the eucharist, and then to lay hands on them for healing. It is an illustration of what American Roman Catholic theologians call the democratisation of the charisms! The ASB confirmation service has a prayer for this:

> Almighty God, whose Holy Spirit equips the Church with a rich variety of gifts, grant that we may use them to bear witness to Christ by lives built on faith and love. (p. 237)

The *Ministry to the Sick* in the Church of England's *Authorised Services* has forms for the laying on of hands with prayer and anointing. It permits a deacon or an authorised lay person to minister the laying on of hands, but it is not clear whether or not they can anoint (in the Roman Church they may).

Marriage

Facing the crisis over the break-up of marriages, more teaching on the spiritual gift of matrimony is essential. Since the marriage of a man and woman is a reflection of the union of Christ and his Church, the married couple constitute an *ecclesiola* – a little fellowship of the Spirit. Unfortunately so often the pronouncements of the Church of England on this subject which are reported in the media are about various aspects for the reform of the divorce laws. Instead of appearing as the spiritual guide of the nation, the Church is depicted as a supporter or an opponent of the reform of the laws on marriage.

Inevitably this means that when church leaders speak about these matters in public, they tend to stress things like fidelity to the marriage vows or the welfare of the children rather than what God can do for us. It is assumed that, speaking to the nation as the established Church, those who hear or read statements and reports are not likely to have faith in Jesus Christ or in the power of the Spirit. The gospel of forgiveness and renewal – the key to all growing relationships – is muted.

Personal renewal in the Holy Spirit spins off into a renewal in personal relationships, beginning with God through Jesus Christ and then to those nearest to us, especially in the community of faith. I have known husbands and wives who, after an experience of baptism in the Spirit, have declared that they seem to find a renewal of their marriage one of the most precious consequences. 'It's like having another and better honeymoon' is a common remark. Every couple should seek to be 'strengthened with every good gift' from God (*ASB Marriage service*). It is surprising how many Christian husbands and wives only begin to pray together after Spirit-baptism and to minister to one another and to their children through spiritual gifts.

The family as a little church is obviously the ideal place for Christian nurture. Not long ago I was speaking to a father about his two teenage children who were showing signs of reluctance about coming to worship in church. 'What we've done sometimes,' he said, 'is to have a eucharist at home round the breakfast table on a Sunday morning. We read the Scriptures, pray, and then I ask God to bless some bread and wine, and we all receive Communion together.'

I did not point out that, as an Anglican layman, he did not have authority to preside at such a service. I simply marvelled at the wisdom of this man in exercising his pastoral and priestly role as the father of the household. Had he asked me what I thought about what he did (which he didn't), I would have had to have said, 'It may not have been a sacrament of the Church of England, because it was not celebrated as laid down by our Church; but I've no doubt whatever that the Lord was with you in the breaking of bread.'

An increasing problem is the pastoral care of those who are

divorced and requests for a second marriage to be blessed in church. There has been a slow acceptance among Anglicans in this country that once a marriage is dead, there is little justification in claiming it is God's will that divorced partners should remain single for the rest of their lives. At the same time, it is also felt that the Church of England should provide some means whereby penitence is expressed for the failures of the past as a preliminary to the remarriage. Although many such remarriages are happier than previous ones, the partners often have to live with what one couple once described to me as 'the ghosts of our past'. A sense of personal guilt for what had happened can linger for years afterwards. An act of penitence followed by prayer for personal renewal in the Holy Spirit, perhaps supported by appropriate sacramental signs, could bring the Lord's mercy and healing in such situations. I have made one or two suggestions for this in Appendix 4.

Religious Life

Some members of religious orders involved with the charismatic renewal have been given a new vision of their vows of celibacy as a spiritual gift. They are fulfilling the word of Jesus Christ that some are called to renounce marriage for the sake of the kingdom. But final vows for the religious life are only taken after a long period when vocations have been tested according to well-tried, traditional methods. This is an exercise in the discernment of charisms which is relevant to other gifts and ministries, too. Indeed, the 'hands on' training for ordination which I described in Chapter 11 is another form of such a novitiate. The vows of the religious life have a sacramental significance in binding the member to the community, as in marriage.

The witness of the religious orders to the virtues of obedience, poverty (that is, detachment from material possessions and chastity as prophetic signs denouncing selfishness, greed and sexual immorality, is a powerful demonstration of the Spirit's power in an age when our culture is rejecting such standards. They can be enormously encouraging to Christian married couples, who are seeking such virtues in their families, as well as to single people, pestered by the pressures of peer groups and the media. It could be argued that it is the abandonment of any proper respect for obedience, poverty and chastity which is at the root of practically everything that is going wrong in our society.

Alongside the older religious orders are the numerous covenant communities and informal extended families which have sprung up since the charismatic renewal has spread. These usually have a shorter existence than the older communities and in most of them the commitment of individual members is only for a number of years. Nevertheless, the same principles apply to their lifestyles, taking their inspiration from the picture of the earliest apostolic community we are given in Acts 2:42–7 – the first great witness to the Pentecostal gift. When I was in such a community at Whatcombe House in Dorset, we found the advice behind such classics as the Rule of St Benedict invaluable in sorting out our priorities.

Through their commitment to one another and through their relationships with local Christian congregations, with their neighbourhoods, and with other groups and movements for justice, peace and the integrity of creation, these communities are reminders to us that sacraments and spiritual gifts are for the proclamation of the gospel and the mission of the Church in God's world.

15

Pastoral Futures

We have seen that, in discussing sacraments and spiritual gifts, we are in fact discussing our relationship with Jesus Christ himself. He comes to us through the sacred doors of the sacraments and the graceful power of the charisms.

A sacrament is a sign of receiving, through faith, the love of God which is being offered us through the celebration of the sacramental sign. Since that love between the Father and the Son is shared with us by the Holy Spirit, then it is the Spirit who gives life to the sacraments. He is 'Lord and giver of life', as we say in the Nicene Creed.

But the Spirit also gives life to us through his comings and his gifts. We are anointed by Jesus to become his Spirit-filled servants ministering in his power. That power is manifested when, according to his will, we step out in faith to minister to others in his name. They also receive the love of God through the charisms – his word, his forgiveness, his deliverance, his healing, his guidance, his equipping – whatever they need and whatever they are ready to accept. There is, then, an intimate connection between sacraments and charisms – a connection in which the boundaries are blurred, as they must be in any loving relationship between persons.

And the place where this relationship is found is within the Church. There the sacraments assure believers of God's presence and grace 'until he comes' (1 Corinthians 11:26); there the gifts of the Spirit build up the body of Christ 'until we all reach unity in the faith and in the knowledge of the Son of God and become mature, attaining to the whole measure of the fulness of Christ' (Ephesians 4:13). To regard God's people only as a sacramental institution is just as limiting as to regard them only as a charismatic fellowship. The sacramental and the charismatic belong together, expressing our relationship with God through his incarnate Son who enfolds us with his life-giving Spirit.

This has been the scope of our discussion. Yet I feel it would be incomplete without some attempt to apply it pragmatically to the ministry and mission of the Church of England today. We have noted some of the ways our Church is beginning to follow the Spirit in re-ordering its sacramental teaching and practice. The discerning of spiritual gifts is one of the reasons for that re-ordering. But lessons are being learned through other means as well.

Social and cultural changes have their effect on our discernment and practice, as we see the Creator Spirit active in the world around us. The various ways in which the eucharist is celebrated is an example of this. Congregations and groups may use one of the traditional settings in a neo-Gothic church, or the latest songs from a Christian rock compact disc in a youth centre. There are other examples. The ministry of reconciliation often includes counselling with prayers for inner healing. The spread of the healing ministry is partly a response to the contemporary concern for holistic medicine. Equality of the sexes is a factor in decisions about the ordination of women. And so on . . .

We are also learning from other faiths – principally Judaism. Celebrations of a Christian passover supper demonstrate how a meal can be sacramental with or without a eucharist. Peter and Michele Guinness of St Thomas' Church, Lancaster, are among those who are introducing these celebrations to parishes. Messianic Jews may teach us more along these lines in the future.

Other lessons are being absorbed through local ecumenism. Baptism in the name of the Trinity is now accepted by all, with the exception of the baptism of infants by the Baptists. Eucharistic hospitality is allowed by everyone, even by the Roman Church in certain cases. The Free Churches have for many years 'recognised and regarded' one another's ordained ministers, and since the eighties canon B44, one of the 'ecumenical canons' of the Church of England, allows ministers of other denominations within local ecumenical projects to preside at eucharists using Anglican rites.

Local ecumenism assists our discernment of spiritual gifts in other traditions. Ordinary Anglican layfolk who belong to united congregations raise questions which challenge our presuppositions. They ask: 'Why should a URC eucharist be considered different from ours?' 'Why is a Church of England priest not the same as a Baptist min: ter?' 'Why should the oversight of the Methodist chairman of district not be accepted as the same as the oversight of a diocesan bishop?'

Questions like these reveal how closely sacraments are interwoven with the institutional nature of the Church. As we struggle to work together in ecumenical congregations, we find the structure of the Church of England a source of frustration. Certain canons, regulations and customs which seem perfectly acceptable within an Anglican milieu, suddenly become stumbling-blocks when we are trying to worship, minister and witness together.

I am not, of course, advocating a free-for-all. Decisions have to be made about the administration of the sacraments and the discerning of spiritual gifts, and some of these decisions have to be embodied in the Church's canon law and other regulations. To allow the sacraments to be administered haphazardly, and spiritual gifts to be exercised without control, would create chaos – the very opposite of the orderliness and unity which are marks of the holy people of God. Scripture and church history teach that all too well.

But these decisions have to be reviewed in the light of the missionary and ecumenical situation as it is now. They have to take into account the fact that society is very different from what it was when certain canons were agreed, and that the Christian community to which they relate is becoming wider than the Church of England.

Canons and Change

We have to remember that canon law originated in the need for the Church to lay down what *should not* be done, rather than what *should* be done. In the early centuries, councils of bishops were called to settle matters of dispute and to decide what they considered should be the norm (which is what 'canon' means) in administering sacraments and discerning gifts. Now some of those norms are changing and our regulations should change with them – though always under the judgement of the basic principles of Christian belief and practice revealed in the Scriptures.

An illustration of this is the ordination of women. Women have exercised leadership roles in the Church from apostolic times. But it was not until the beginning of this century that they were ordained in the Free Churches to preach and to minister the sacraments. This innovation gradually influenced Anglicans, and different provinces round the world began to follow the Free Churches' lead. The Church of England ordained its first women to the presbyterate in the spring of 1994.

It is well-known that a substantial minority of Anglicans refuse to accept this change. Some of them are my friends, and I respect their views. But I have to say that, after years of working with women ministers in other Churches – including some in the Roman Church – I believe such ordinations are a prophetic step. I also believe that what we have done will eventually be recognised as prophetic, too, by the Roman Church and then by the Orthodox Churches.

Another illustration is Christian initiation. Since the Reformation, Christian congregations who baptise believers have been a constant challenge to those who baptised infants. Up until this century, it was still possible to maintain theologically that indiscriminate infant baptism was an appropriate way of ministering the sacrament in a Christian country. But that argument no longer convinces many. The aims of the Baptism Reform Movement are becoming widely accepted, and a small but increasing number of Anglicans are postponing the initiation of their children until they are old enough to profess a personal faith in Jesus Christ.

In a missionary situation, the individual has to depend more on his or her personal faith, because the supports of a christianised society are no longer there. Being a Christian in England today is more like being a Christian in the apostolic age. This, perhaps, is why the picture of the Church in the Acts of the Apostles is so relevant to us.

Church membership is becoming more ecumenical and charismatic (in the theological sense) as women and men are equipped by the Spirit to work for the kingdom of God in the midst of a secular society. Although the sacrament of baptism will, I imagine, be administered to infants of Christian families for the foreseeable future, the numbers of babies being baptised will decline, assisted indirectly by the fall-off in the demand for baptism among non-church families. Christian initiation is rightly becoming a more demanding business, both for the parents of baptised infants and for believers seeking baptism.

Proposals to revive the catechumenate, described in Chapter 8, are a response to the secularisation of society. The casualness of much Anglican preparation for baptism and confirmation in the past has resulted in what Robert Warren calls a 'bolt-on spirituality' – that is, the adoption by individuals of certain Christian doctrines and practices that are added to an existing lifestyle, which itself is formed by the culture we live in, not by the Spirit in us.

But with more teenagers and adults seeking faith through successful evangelism, it is necessary to teach them that being a Christian disciple nowadays means being prepared to enter a counter-culture. Biblical teaching about a new creation and separateness from the world has taken on a new significance. There is much seeking after an active holiness, which does not separate Christians from care and responsibility in society but which enables them to become more Christlike within it.

But the biggest lesson which the Church of England has to learn from other denominations – and especially from the New Churches – is how to realise within her life and structures what is called the 'Ephesians 4' model of ministries. The association of sacrament and charism implied by this text is a radical one indeed for us.

Ephesians 4

I was once asked by a Pentecostal minister where the apostles, prophets, evangelists, pastors and teachers were in the Church of England. When I stumblingly explained the apostolic succession of bishops, priests and deacons, he listened patiently and then described how the Ephesian ministries were emerging in his church. They had apostles, prophets, evangelists, pastors and teachers ministering among their members. 'We're more interested in apostolic success than apostolic succession,' he said crisply.

I felt crushed! But, looking back on that conversation, I don't think I need have been. It's the manifestation of those gifts in the Christian community that matters, not the titles attached to the offices of those who minister them. When we look round the Church of England, we can see these gifts being exercised to some degree.

The bishops have a sort of apostolic ministry, when they are not swamped by the bureaucratic demands. The ministry of prophets has been recognised among individuals and groups who recall us to aspects of the gospel which we are neglecting, and who speak out and act in the cause of justice and peace. The Decade of Evangelism is encouraging us to share the gospel more than we have done before. Many clergy and lay people are pastors and teachers.

But, having said that, certain ministries need strengthening and certain offices need developing. Prophecy, for example, may be manifested locally more than we expect. David Pytches discusses this in *Prophecy in the Local Church* (1993). He points out that prophecy is a ministry which challenges our committee-ridden assumptions about decision-making: 'Our congregations certainly need a dynamic communication from God today, for knowing and doing his will' (p. 3). More parishes are learning how simple gifts of prophecy can clarify their priorities.

The office of an evangelist needs greater recognition. Church Army officers are the only evangelists in the Church of England licensed for this ministry. Certain parish priests seem to be happier evangelising than pastoring. It is said that in any congregation there are probably about ten per cent who are gifted in sharing the gospel with others. The Northern Association of Evangelists has a membership of about fifty – some of them Anglicans. I do not see why Christians with such gifts should not be ordained as presbyter-evangelists.

Baptism in the Spirit is enabling many to enter into renewed and fresh ministries of teaching and pastoring, but specialisation also seems to be common. A ministry of spiritual direction requires some pastoring and teaching skills, but not to the same extent as in shepherding a congregation or lecturing a course. Again, presbyteral ordination may be appropriate for laypersons fulfilling these ministries in some cases. Taking all this into consideration, Anglicans have to admit that the Ephesians 4 pattern does not sit easily with the ordained ministry as we have inherited it.

Open Ordinations

One important lesson our ecumenical experiences can teach us is how to throw open the pastoral leadership of the Church of England to gifted women and men so that evangelists, teachers and other ministries are released.

It has become clear that the English diocese is far too large to be the basic unit of ecclesiastical oversight, and that the parish is too restrictive as a geographical patch of pastoral care. The Church requires unitary structure, flexible and related to the structures of other denominations, in which deaneries would become areas of episcopal oversight, like the slimline dioceses in other parts of the Anglican Communion, and parishes, while retaining their historic names, would be stripped of their legal entity.

Present-day diocesan machinery would be dismantled. Networking rather than geography would be the basis of Christian relationships. Bishops would be restored to their original ministry of pastors of the pastors in local congregations. The present development of team and group ministries would be extended to help us to move away from the one-man-band model of the past.

To service such a pattern of pastoral care and mission, ordination must be freed from the paralysing effect of the doctrine of sacramental character and the complicated bondage of legal status. These have prevented bishops from ordaining men and women to voluntary eldership as freely as in, say, the United Reformed Church.

I have suggested that the locally ordained ministry is a valuable response to this need. Sadly, there are still dioceses which have not encouraged the locally ordained ministry. A strange superstition causes the Church of England to regard large numbers of non-stipendiary presbyters as a threat rather than a resource. Yet when I have discussed this with ordained elders in the URC and in the Church of Scotland, they have been mystified by Anglican hesitations. They have told me that, although their ordination to eldership is permanent, few of them regard this as a ministry which they should exercise for the rest of their lives. Many of them are elders for a period of time; then they return to what Anglicans would call a 'lay' status without any sense of personal or spiritual diminution.

Initiation of locally ordained ministries could be the key for enabling a wider use of charisms of pastoral leadership. Congregations discerning these gifts among members – in 'elders', pastoral assistants and other lay readers – should press for this. The guidelines issued by the bishops for training locally ordained ministers liberate us from the over-academic approach to training to make this possible.

Rather than giving permission for lay presidency at eucharists (a proposal which is likely to create as much debate as the ordination of women has done), bishops should ordain women and men with leadership gifts and license them temporarily (after appropriate instruction) to fulfil that role. Congregations in vacant parishes should be invited to nominate candidates for this. That would retain the ordering of the sacraments in the traditional way and do much to obliterate the clergy-line which everyone is complaining about. What matters in authorising a person to preside at the eucharist is not just the ordination but also the bishop's licence. It does not matter that the sacramental character remains with such persons once their licences are withdrawn.

If I were to say more about the pastoral futures of the Church of England, I should find myself writing another book! But I want to add that, while we should welcome change, we should not do so uncritically. Each new development must be tested. Does it aid the Church in its kingdom work and mission? Is it consistent with the Church's origins (is it apostolic)? Does it equip all the saints to be servants? Does it build up the body of Christ – the whole body ecumenically? Does it enable the believers together to grow into a maturity that is Christlike and Spirit-filled? In seeking the Lord's will in these matters, we shall find guidance in what the Spirit has led the Church to institute in the past as well as in the prophetic signs of the present.

Sacraments and Charisms until the Kingdom

To conclude, then, the sacraments and the gifts of the Spirit have been handed down to us until Jesus Christ comes again and the age of the kingdom dawns in its fulness. Then sacraments and charisms will pass away. Only Love will remain.

Until then, for those who receive baptism, the Spirit makes real the washing away of obstacles to unity with God and the power to transform human relationships (which may be very fragile) into an expression of the love of God.

Confirmation through anointing and/or the laying on of hands is a further sign of the equipping by the Spirit for personal ministries to others.

The ministry of reconciliation, now often administered with the laying on of hands, is the means through which those who have fallen into serious sin and weakened their unity with God and with the Church, are assured of God's forgiveness and of reconciliation with their sisters and brothers. It brings a personal renewing in the Spirit, liberating the baptised to minister with greater thankfulness as those who have known forgiveness in themselves.

Anointing and the laying on of hands are signs of the healing ministry of Jesus Christ among the sick. Although usually through no fault of the patient, sickness is a sign of the disorder and sinfulness of God's world, and in ministering to the sick we invoke the healing gifts of the Spirit through the use of these sacramental signs for the restoration of wholeness.

Marriage symbolises and the Spirit enables Christian couples to live in a human love which is in itself a sign – a living sacrament, even – of divine love. Their loving commitment to each other is a tiny manifestation of the loving commitment of Jesus Christ to us in the new covenant, and of the gift of the Spirit which makes it possible to live faithfully to him and to one another.

Ordination recognises and the Spirit bestows on the recipients authority to exercise for the Church those charisms of pastoral leadership which are discerned by the Christian community, uniting us and guiding us in Christ's own ministry as he leads his disciples on the way to his kingdom.

And, as the focus of them all, the eucharist, the sacrament of the sacraments, celebrates and the Spirit puts us in touch with that love of God which is never withdrawn, always forgiving, even when sinned against, and always renewed and strengthened. The Supper of the Lord deepens the unity we have with Jesus Christ and with one another in the Spirit, sharing in his relationship to the Father, and the sacrifice which made such unity possible.

Furthermore, our use of bread and wine as a sacramental sign of Christ's body and blood (however we interpret this) is an anticipation of the future transformation of all material things by the Spirit. The eucharist is, then, also a prophetic symbol of the heavenly banquet when space and time no longer limit our ability to be present to each other in Jesus Christ.

The relationship between sacraments and charisms demonstrates how the institutional and the charismatic within the Christian community complement, test and support each other; but where the Spirit leads, the institution must follow.

We are members of a Church in which the sacraments are being revived by the Holiness-Pentecostal spirituality coming to us in the charismatic renewal and allied to other impulses of the Spirit – the biblical, liturgical and ecumenical movements.

Through an interweaving of both the sacraments as we have received them and the full spectrum of New Testament gifts restored through the renewal, we are encountering Jesus Christ afresh as we worship the Father in him, and as he sends us out to live and proclaim the kingdom of God together in the power of his Spirit.

Appendix 1

(See page 38.)

The medieval Schoolmen were influenced by Aristotle's philosophical vocabulary which used pairs of terms such as 'substance' and 'accident', and 'matter' and 'form', to analyse the nature of reality. It was from the former pair that the doctrine of transubstantiation arose – that the bread and the wine retained their outward qualities ('accidents') but their inner reality was changed ('trans-substantiated') into the body and blood of Christ.

The second pair of terms were adapted to explain the way in which the grace of God came through the sacraments. The gestures and objects used were the 'matter' of the sacrament, and the words spoken to accompany them were the 'form'. Eventually these definitions became more precise and embodied in conciliar definitions and Roman Catholic canons. So bread, wine, oil, and the laying on of hands were 'matter'; 'I baptise you . . .', 'I absolve you . . .', 'Receive the Holy Spirit . . .' were the 'form'. The use of the words of institution within the eucharistic prayer also came to be regarded as the 'form' for the mass.

In restoring the use of the sacraments in the Church of England, the Tractarians and their successors have tried to apply these definitions to Anglican sacramental teaching and practice.

Appendix 2

THE APOSTOLIC SUCCESSION

(See page 85.)

Since ordination with the laying on of episcopal hands became general in the early centuries, it followed that as bishops succeeded one another, that gesture came to be valued as a sign of continuity. Apostolic succession originally meant a continuity in teaching the doctrine of the apostles as well as a continuity in pastoral care; but the importance of the gesture was magnified when the authority of individual bishops was challenged by schismatics or heretics. Thus the doctrine of apostolic succession became embedded in the sacramental theology of the medieval Church and regarded as an essential part of the 'matter' of orders. The Tractarians appealed to this doctrine when they reminded Church of England clergy that they were priests of the Catholic Church in a succession of ministry stretching back to the time of the apostles.

When an appeal was made to the Roman Church to declare whether or not Anglican orders were valid, the claim that this apostolic succession had been broken during the ordination of Elizabeth I's bishops was one of the arguments put forward in the papal encyclical *Apostolicae curae* (1896) declaring Anglican orders 'absolutely null and utterly void'.

Catholic Anglicans rejected schemes of reunion with the non-episcopal Church which did not safeguard the apostolic succession; but in recent years theologians have given it less prominence in ecumenical discussions.

Appendix 3

(See page 106.)
I have taken as my first example Eucharistic Prayer D from *Patterns for Worship* (pp. 250–1). In the instructions which accompany this prayer, the Liturgical Commission has directed that the proper preface should be one of those which are provided in the 'Praise' section of the book, so I have taken the one numbered 64.27 ('Kingdom, Ascension' – p. 194).

The Commission also printed the song, 'Holy, holy, holy is the Lord', as an alternative form of the Sanctus (p. 252), which suggests that what I am proposing was not far from their minds, either! In these examples the words said or sung by the congregation are printed in **bold**, and the songs and choruses (all taken from *Songs and Hymns of Fellowship*) are in *italics*.

As you read the first example, imagine that the words of the prayer and the singing flow steadily from one to the other with no sense of rush, but rather as an extended symphony of praise to God.

Example 1

The Lord is here.
His Spirit is with us.
Lift up your hearts.
We lift them to the Lord.
Let us give thanks to the Lord our God.
It is right to give him thanks and praise.

O Lord our God, how majestic is Your name.
The earth is filled with Your glory. . . .

Chorus:

*We will magnify. . . **

(Phil Lawson Johnston, *Songs and Hymns of Fellowship* 409)

And now we give you thanks because
Jesus has been given all authority
in heaven and on earth
to present to you, his Father,
a kingdom of truth, holiness and everlasting love.

So, with angels and archangels, and all the company of heaven,
we praise you for ever, singing:

Holy, holy, holy is the Lord;
Holy is the Lord God almighty!
Holy, holy, holy is the Lord;
Holy is the Lord God almighty!
Who was, and is, and is to come,
Holy, holy, holy is the Lord!

Jesus, Jesus, Jesus is the Lord. . .

Worthy, worthy, worthy is the Lord. . .

Glory, glory, glory to the Lord. . .

(Author unknown, SHF 166.)

Praise and thanks to you, Father in heaven:
on the night before he died
your Son Jesus Christ took bread and wine.
He gave thanks and said
This is my body, given for you.
This is my blood, shed for the forgiveness of sins.

Jesus, Name above all names,
Beautiful Saviour,
Glorious Lord; Emmanuel, God is with us,
Blessed Redeemer, Living Word.

(Naida Hearn, SHF 288)

Pour out your Holy Spirit
as we bring before you these gifts

and remember his sacrifice
made once for all on the cross.
Feed us with his body and blood,
that we may live and grow in him.
Through him we worship you, Father almighty,
in songs of everlasting praise.

We worship and adore thee,
Bowing down before Thee,
songs of praises singing,
Hallelujahs ringing:
Hallelujah, Hallelujah,
Hallelujah. Amen.

(Author unknown, SHF 594)

Example 2

Another way of incorporating modern songs is to use them as
accompanying choral music to the recitation of the prayer. For
this either the president has to speak clearly above the softly
sung choruses, or he has to project his voice using the public
address system carefully.

Take, for example, the beginning of Alternative Eucharistic
Prayer A (p. 239). This preface uses passages from the Old
Testament in a manner reminiscent of a Jewish table blessing.
It is also in the form of a versicle and response.

Daniel Daniels' chorus, *You are the Vine* (SHF 633), draws
on texts from John 13:34–5 and 15:1–11, Christ's discourse at
the Last Supper. The effect is something like this:

We celebrate together
  the gifts and grace of God.
We take this bread,
We take this wine,
to follow his example,
and to obey his command.

Lift up your hearts.
We lift them up to the Lord.
Let us give thanks
  to the Lord our God

**It is right to give him
thanks and praise.**

Blessed are you, Lord,
   God of the universe,
you bring forth bread from the   *You are the Vine.*
   earth.
Blessed be God for ever.
Blessed are you, Lord,
   God of the universe,
You create the fruit of the   *We are the branches.*
   vine.
Blessed be God for ever.
The created universe praises
   you,
   its creator.
Sun and rain, hills and rivers
   praise you.   *Keep us abiding in You.*
Blessed be God for ever.
The fruit of the earth itself
   praises you:
Wheat and grape,
   this bread and wine we
   have,
are part of the riches of your   *etc. . . .**
   earth.
**You are worthy,
   our Lord and God,
to receive glory and honour
   and power,
for you created all things,
   and through your will
they have their being.**
You made us in your image,
   and went on loving us,
even when we turned against
   you.
You loved us so much
   you gave up your Son

* Copyright restrictions prevent me from printing the full texts of
these songs.

that we may no longer be
  slaves to sins
but rise to life with him....
  etc.

The music lends itself to being softly sung. The guitar group could sing this quietly as background music while the president and congregation take their parts in the eucharistic prayer.

Once a congregation has become familiar with this form of praise, it can develop in many different ways. One thing to remember is to vary the songs so that they do not become yet another 'setting' for the eucharist.

Appendix 4

(See page 125.)

SERVICES AFTER DIVORCE

How to plan a liturgical act which marks the end of a marriage is not easy, and I am not altogether sure that it can be done. Some years ago the United Reformed Church issued a service for the release of marriage vows. It is not much used, because the concept of being released from such vows is highly controversial.

I know of two similar services which I will describe, not because I am commending them for general use, but because I think they are interesting attempts to meet this particular need.

The first I only heard about. A divorcing couple met in church with some friends and members of the congregation, and formally confessed the failure of their marriage to God and to one another. Prayers were then said for them, they gave each other and everyone else the peace, and then they went their separate ways. I admire their honesty and humility; but I would have thought that any couple who were prepared to do that would also be prepared to seek reconciliation.

The second I attended three or four years ago. It was a service along similar lines, though with only one of the divorced partners present.

I had known Ann and Malcolm (not their real names) for a long time. They had been faithful Christians for years. Then, for reasons which I need not explain, Malcolm left his wife and they were divorced.

Ann invited about twenty of her personal friends, including me, and members of the congregation to meet her in church with the minister who had stood by her through these difficult years. We sat in a circle round the communion table. On the table, propped up on a bookstand, was a large photograph of

Malcolm and Ann taken on their wedding-day. It gave me a strange feeling to see them looking so young and happy in the picture. I wondered why the photo was there. I was soon to find out.

We were handed a sheet of paper headed: 'A service to mark the end of the marriage of Malcolm and Ann Smith, and the single state of Ann.'

The minister began: 'We are gathered here in the presence of God to acknowledge the end of the marriage of Malcolm and Ann, to give thanks for all that was good in it, to recognise and seek forgiveness for what was wrong; and to affirm Ann's single state and her desire to commit the whole of her life to God's service.'

We stood and sang a hymn which, we were told, had been sung at Malcolm's and Ann's wedding. It was followed by a prayer in which thanksgiving was mingled with penitence. Then the minister moved to the table, facing the photograph.

'We give thanks,' he said, 'that we can know and share the forgiveness Christ brings. Now we offer to God this marriage as a completed and closed volume.'

He raised his hand and moved the photograph so that it came apart into two parts. We now saw that it had been ripped in such a way that the figures of the bride and the bridegroom were separated.

'This picture is already torn,' said the minister, 'not cleanly and painlessly, for some of Ann has stayed with Malcolm, and some of Malcolm has stayed with Ann. That is the way it is. As changed and changing people, they set out on separate paths. Wherever these lead, the love of God can be found there.'

The service continued with a Scripture reading, prayers for Ann, and another hymn. After the service Ann, trying to smile through her tears, moved round giving us the peace. We gave her a hug, shook hands with the minister, and went home.

Both these services tried to bring the situation created by the divorces before God within the fellowship of the Church. The second one I have described helped Ann to offer her guilt and grief to the Lord, the simple use of the photograph acting as a powerful symbol. That service also helped me and the others accept her – and her to accept us – as she began her life without Malcolm.

Notes

Chapter 1

1. This chapter owes much to the relevant entries in the *Dictionary of Pentecostal and Charismatic Movements*, ed. Stanley M. Burgess and Gary B. McGee (1988), to James R. Goff, *Fields White Unto Harvest: Charles F. Parham and the Missionary Origins of Pentecostalism* (1988), and to the review of the second book by Augustus Cerille in *Pneuma: The Journal of the Society for Pentecostal Studies*, Volume 15:1 (Spring 1993), pp. 77–88.

Chapter 2

1. Anglican Renewal Ministries, 45 Friar Gate, Derby DE1 1DA.
2. Peter Brierley, *Christian England* (1991), pp. 127ff.

Chapter 3

1. *The Works of St Bernard of Clairvaux*: Treatise 1, Cistercian Fathers Series no. 1, p. 144.
2. *Symeon the New Theologian: The Discourses* (*Classics of Western Spirituality*, 1980), p. 17.
3. *Alternative Service Book*, p. 450.
4. From his *Letters on Spiritual Virtues*, quoted in Richard Foster and James Bryan Smith, *Devotional Classics* (1993), p. 349.
5. From *The Works of Jonathan Edwards*, Vol. 2, quoted in *Devotional Classics*, p. 33
6. *The Works of John Wesley*, vol.1 quoted in Colin William's *John Wesley's Theology Today* (1960), p. 98.
7. Quoted in Frederick Dale Bruner, *A Theology of the Holy Spirit* (1970), p. 46.

Chapter 4

1. Commentary on Psalm 99, quoted in Eddie Ensley, *Sounds of Wonder: A Popular History of Speaking in Tongues in the Catholic Tradition* (1977), p. 8.
2. Quoted in Ensley, *op. cit.*, p. 66.
3. Evelyn Underhill, *Jacopone da Todi* (1919), pp. 77–8.
4. Watson E. Mills (ed.), *Speaking in Tongues* (1986), p. 342.

5. Karl Rahner, 'Religious Enthusiasm and the Experience of Grace' in *Theological Investigations* XVI (1979), pp. 35–59.

Chapter 5
1. In this chapter I have relied especially on Joseph Martos, *Doors to the Sacred: A Historical Introduction to Sacraments in the Christian Church* (1981); Hans Kung, *The Church* (1967); and Harding Meyer and Lukas Vischer, *Growth in Agreement: Reports and Agreed Statements on Ecumenical Conversations on a World Level* (1984).

Chapter 6
1. Martin Dudley and Geoffrey Rowell, *The Oil of Gladness* (1993), p. 134.

Chapter 7
1. Francis Sullivan, *Charisms and Charismatic Renewal* (1982), p. 63, his italics.
2. *We Believe in the Holy Spirit* (1991), p. 48. For a balanced review, see H. I. Lederle, *Treasures Old and New: Interpretations of Spirit-Baptism in the Charismatic Renewal Movement* (1988).

Chapter 9
1. Henry Bettensen, *Documents of the Christian Church* (1943), pp. 443–4.
2. I am indebted to John N. Collins for this example (see his article, 'The Language of Ministry' in *One in Christ*, 1991, p. 241).

Chapter 10
1. Edward Schillebeckx discusses this historical development in *Ministry* (1981).
2. Paul F. Bradshaw, *The Study of Liturgy*, ed. Cheslyn Jones, Geoffrey Wainwright, Edward Yarnold and Paul Bradshaw, (1992), p. 355.

Chapter 12
1. Pierre Gelineau, *The Liturgy Today and Tomorrow* (1978), p. 90.

Chapter 13
1. Some of the material in this chapter was used in *Anglican Renewal*'s theological inset, 'Skepsis', No. 45 (1991).

Index